MW00986222

A Sufi Rule for Novices

HARVARD MIDDLE EASTERN STUDIES, 17

A Sufi Rule for Novices

Kitāb Ādāb al-Murīdīn of Abū al-Najīb al-Suhrawardī

AN ABRIDGED TRANSLATION
AND INTRODUCTION by
Menahem Milson

Harvard University Press
Cambridge, Massachusetts
and London, England
1975

Library of Congress Catalog Card Number 742–7750
ISBN 0–674–85400–4 (cloth)
ISBN 0–674–85403–9 (paper)
Printed in the United States of America

Preface

A Sufi Rule for Novices presents an outline of Sufism as seen by one of the great Sufi masters. This volume consists of two parts: an abridged translation of Abū al-Najīb al-Suhrawardī's *Kitāb Ādāb al-Murīdīn* (the book of rules for novices) and an introduction including a general survey of Sufism and a study of Suhrawardī's work.

Kitāb Ādāb al-Murīdīn, which is available in numerous Arabic manuscripts, has not yet appeared in print. My edition of the Arabic text is about to be published by the Institute of Asian and African Studies of the Hebrew University of Jerusalem. The first detailed study of this work is presented here.

Abū al-Najīb al-Suhrawardī may be considered a typical representative of orthodox Sufism, combining legal and theological scholarship with mystical devotion, retirement from the world (as a temporary stage), and constant dedication to teaching and guiding the many. Thus, through a detailed study of this individual Sufi master we may grasp more concretely the nature of orthodox Sufism and its role in the formation of medieval Islam.

I have attempted to determine the place of Suhrawardī's book in Sufi literature and the particular purpose of the author in this composition. My conclusions concerning the relation between Suhrawardī's *Kitāb Ādāb al-Murīdīn* and other books, both earlier and later, are based on comparative data which are presented in detail in the apparatus of my edition of the Arabic text.

The abridged translation is intended primarily for the reader who does not know Arabic. I hope, however, that it may also be useful to the reader who will be able to refer to the Arabic text. The abridgment made in the translation is minimal. I have omitted only sayings and anecdotes that do not seem essential for the understanding of the particular section and that could be omitted without impairing the structure of Suhrawardī's composition. In each such instance, the abridgment is indicated by a short notice enclosed in parentheses. Quotations from the Quran are generally not translated, and the parenthetical reference cites the chapter and verse according to the standard Egyptian edition of the Quran. Parentheses are thus used in a special way to indicate abridgment, in addition to their other conventional uses. Brackets are used to enclose various types of additions to the text: words or phrases added in the translation when the Arabic original seems elliptical, subheadings given in the translation to various sections, and fuller forms of some names to facilitate their identification.

In a preliminary stage, this book formed part of a doctoral dissertation prepared under the supervision of the late Sir Hamilton A. R. Gibb. I should like to record here my debt of gratitude to Professor Gibb for his help and encouragement. I am greatly indebted to Professor M. J. Kister of the Hebrew University of Jerusalem, who called my attention to *Kitāb Ādāb al-Murīdīn*. My indebtedness to Kister goes far beyond this, for it was he who first taught me to read Arabic and initiated me in the study of Islam in general and Sufism in particular.

Menahem Milson

The Hebrew University
Jerusalem, 1975

Contents

Introduction 1

Sufism and Sufi Orders
Abū al-Najīb al-Suhrawardī—A Biographical Note
Kitāb Ādāb al-Murīdīn—A Sufi Rule

Rules for the Novice 27

Kitāb Ādāb al-Murīdīn, An Abridged Translation

Bibliography 85
Glossary 89

A Sufi Rule for Novices

Introduction

Sufism, Islamic mysticism, has attracted a good deal of scholarly interest on the part of Western students of Islam, and consequently a considerable number of books on this subject, both general surveys and monographic studies, are available today. Thanks to these works I need not attempt the impossible task of condensing a description of Sufism into a few pages of introduction to the present volume. Rather, I shall present a brief outline to place this book in the necessary perspective of the history of Sufism and Sufi orders, while referring the reader to general expositions of this subject for further information.[1]

[1]See the relatively short but comprehensive survey by Marijan Molé, *Les Mystiques musulmans* (Paris: Presses Universitaires de France, 1965). Molé appends to each chapter a very useful bibliographic note. See also A. J. Arberry, *Ṣufism: An Account of the Mystics of Islam* (London: George Allen and Unwin, Ltd., 1950; 2nd printing, 1956). G.-C. Anawati and L. Gardet, *Mystique musulmane* (Paris: J. Vrin, 1961), provides a more detailed exposition than the two books mentioned above. H. A. R. Gibb, *Mohammedanism*, 2nd ed. (London: Oxford University Press, 1964), includes chapters on Sufism and the Sufi orders that present an excellent overall picture. Arberry's *An Introduction to the History of Ṣūfism* (London: Longmans, Green and Co., 1942), is an account of Western scholarship in the field of Sufism until about 1940; it contains much bibliographic information. On the history of Sufi orders see J. Spencer Trimingham, *The Sufi Orders in Islam* (Oxford: Oxford University Press, 1971).

The fundamental reference work on Islam is *The Encyclopaedia of Islam*, 4 vols. and supplement (Leiden: E. J. Brill, and London: Luzac & Co., 1913–1938), henceforth cited *EI* and *EI Supp.*, and its new edition (1960–). Henceforth cited EI^2.

Sufism and Sufi Orders

The Quran and subsequent Islamic thought teach that God is the transcendental Creator and hence the master (*al-rabb*) and that man is His creature and hence His bondservant (*ʿabd*). Indeed, so fundamental is the concept of man's servitude to the divine Master that *ʿabd* is a very common designation for man in Islamic religious writing. Consciousness of the terrible abyss between the eternal all-powerful God and man the mortal, placed in this created, perishable world, is ever present in the Quran. However, the Quran also confirms that God did not forsake man, for in His bounty He established a covenant between Himself and man which—in its final manifestation in history—is the covenant between Himself and the Islamic community of believers (*al-umma*).

According to this covenant, the believer, as servant, is required to obey the Master's commands implicitly, that is, to observe the divine law (*sharīʿa*) as revealed in the Quran and the subsequent sources of Islamic jurisprudence. This is the sole means of contact, revealed to all and available to all, between man and God.[2] Arduous study of the law therefore acquires supreme religious importance, for it is through jurisprudence that one can aspire to learn, as fully and as exactly as possible, what God requires.

Yet this type of religious attitude could not satisfy all religious minds, and from the earliest days of Islam we find those whose religious fervor was manifested in ways which go beyond the requirements of the *sharīʿa*.

To be sure, this does not suggest that those persons neglected the divine law. Quite the contrary. Being painfully aware of

[2] I am greatly indebted for my understanding of the relationship between the classical prophetic phase of religion and the mystical phase to Gershom G. Scholem's incisive observations on this matter. See his *Major Trends in Jewish Mysticism* (London: Thames & Hudson, 1955), pp. 7–10.

human imperfection, they held that man could not possibly go too far in attempting to carry out God's orders. Hence, one of the characteristics of those early Muslim pietists was their utmost scrupulosity (*wara'*) in observing the rules of the *sharī'a* in ritual and social matters. Earnestly impressed with the Quranic teaching about the impending Day of Judgment and the imminent doom of this world, early Muslim pietists directed themselves to prepare for the hereafter. They were appalled by the worldly attitude of many of the ruling elite of the Caliphate, who were more preoccupied with the expansion of Islamic dominion than with their ultimate fate and who enjoyed the riches which were afforded them. For their part, those pious men shunned the world and its affairs, contemptuous of its worthlessness and wary of its temptations. Asceticism (*zuhd*) was their way of life.

Sufi doctrine, expounded in its mature form in the fourth and fifth centuries A.H.,[3] considers *zuhd* to be one of the primary stages or, to use Sufi terminology, "stations" (*maqāmāt*) along the way which every mystic should traverse.[4] Sufi masters always count the early ascetics as their precursors and mentors. Admittedly, asceticism, as such, is not to be confused with Sufism; however, the connection between the two can hardly be doubted.

The question of the origins of Sufism has long been debated by Western scholars, most of whom, until the last generation, held that the essential ideas of Islamic mysticism had originated from alien, non-Islamic sources.[5] Admittedly, Sufism absorbed a considerable number of heterogenous elements; the influence of Neoplatonism was especially significant. It

[3]A.H. signifies the Islamic era, counting the years, according to the lunar calendar, from the time of Muḥammad's emigration (*hijra*) to Medina in 622 A.D.

[4]See secs. 49 and 66 below.

[5]See a brief account of those views in Arberry's *Introduction*.

should be recognized, however, that the primary sources of Sufism are Islamic, the Quran being first and foremost among them.[6]

The ascetics, who turned their backs on the world, sought guidance from God by repetitive recitation of His word, the Quran. Desiring to have some contact with the divine, they strove to internalize God's words by assiduously pondering their meaning. This process of internalization of the Quran must have induced some of those who were engaged in it occasionally to experience the nearness of God and consequently to form mystical concepts associated with the Quranic text.[7] It is in the circles of such pious ascetics that Sufism evolved.

Much in the tradition of Christian monks and other ascetics in Syria and Egypt, many of the Muslim ascetics chose to wear a frock made of coarse wool (*ṣūf*) as a mark of penitence and renunciation of worldly vanities. The term *ṣūfī* (a person clad in wool) was used as a personal ascriptive appellation in the second century A.H. The plural form *ṣūfiyya* is attested in third-century texts in reference to a group.[8] *Ṣūfī* eventually became the common designation of mystics in Islam. From the adjectival form *sūfī*, the verbal noun *taṣawwuf* was derived, meaning "to be a Sufi" or "to strive to become a Sufi." It is somewhat curious, but not inexplicable, that the term which designates Islamic mysticism (*taṣawwuf*), as distinct from the earlier asceticism (*zuhd*), is in fact derived from one of the characteristic features of the ascetic practice and not from the sphere of mystical theory.[9]

The third century A.H. appears to have been the formative

[6]This view of Sufi origins seems to have been firmly established by L. Massignon in his *Essai sur les origines du lexique technique de la mystique musulmane* (Paris: J. Vrin, 1954) and *La Passion d'al-Ḥallāj* (Paris: P. Geuthner, 1922).

[7]See Massignon, *Essai*, pp. 45–49, and idem, *Passion*, II, 464–467.

[8]See Massignon, *Essai*, pp. 153–155.

[9]This curiosity in the terminology was noted by many Sufi authors.

period in the development of Sufism, when great Sufi masters such as Dhū al-Nūn al-Miṣrī, al-Ḥārith al-Muḥāsibī, Sahl al-Tustarī, Abū Yazīd (Bāyazīd) al-Bisṭāmī, Junayd, and al-Ḥallāj created the modes of mystical practice and theory in Islam.

The next stage in the development of Sufism appears in the Sufi compilations dating from the latter part of the fourth century and the first half of the fifth century A.H. The most notable Sufi books of that period are those of Sarrāj (d. 378/988), Abū Ṭālib al-Makkī (d. 386/996), Kalābādhī (d. 390/1000), Sulamī (d. 421/1021), Abū Nuʿaym al-Iṣfahānī (d. 430/1038), Qushayrī (d. 465/1072), and Hujwīrī (fl. 450/1057). Collectively, the works of these authors attest that something very significant had by then been accomplished, namely, the formation of a Sufi tradition. By Sufi tradition I mean a corpus that included an elaborate technical vocabulary, a list of eminent mystics who are recognized as the founders and authoritative masters of Sufism, a large stock of hagiographic materials, and a common theory of the mystical way (*ṭarīqa*).

The Sufi way of spiritual ascent includes a number of stations in progressive order that the Sufi must traverse under the guidance of his master. The attainment of each station (*maqām*) is believed to be effected by the individual's endeavor. In addition to the stations, there are spiritual states (*aḥwāl*) which inspire the Sufi. These, unlike the stations, do not result from human action or volition but from God's favor; they are regarded as divine gifts. There are, of course, variations in the itinerary of the way, as taught by different masters: the number and order of stations vary, and there are different explanations of the interrelation of state and station. The basic concepts are nonetheless similar.[10]

[10]See a brief account of the doctrine of stations and states in Arberry, *Sufism*, pp. 74–83, and secs. 49–50 below.

The emergence of this doctrine of stations and states in the fourth century A.H. must represent extensive effort in collecting, combining, systematizing, and, to a large extent, synthesizing the teachings of the great mystics of the earlier generations.

Since the fifth century A.H., Sufism has attracted a large following in all strata of society. This development appears to have resulted from the need which many Muslims felt to enrich emotionally their religious life. Such need was experienced not only by the uneducated, who were naturally debarred from the intellectual satisfaction that could be derived from juristic and theological studies, but also by many of the religious scholars (*ʿulamāʾ*)—guardians of the divine law of *sharīʿa*. Laymen and *ʿulamāʾ* alike adopted Sufism to satisfy that need.

This is rather remarkable, for the mystical outlook embodied in Sufism is radically different from that religiosity which, unremittingly mindful of God's transcendence, is focused on His law. It is the inner mystical aspect of religion which is the main concern of the Sufi rather than the external juristic aspect, the esoteric "true reality" (*ḥaqīqa*) rather than the exoteric *sharīʿa*.

Yet Sufis did not constitute a sect; with few exceptions they remained within the fold. They have always regarded themselves, and have been regarded by most other Muslims, as part of the orthodox (*sunnī*) community, a concept which is expressed by the Arabic idiom *ahl al-sunna wa-'l-jamāʿa*—"those who adhere to the tradition and the community." Indeed, the Sufis held that they were the very core of that community. This idea is expressed in one of the best known Sufi compendiums in these words: "The most excellent of the Muslim community, who keep their respiration with God and safeguard their heart from the intrusions of heedlessness, have singled themselves out with the name of Sufism; and this name has become famous in reference to these great men before the year two hundred A.H."[11]

There are, it seems, two characteristics of Sufism which made it possible for its adherents to avoid schism between themselves and nonmystical traditional Islam and to attract a large following. The first is Sufi insistence on the observance of the law: no one could aspire to attain the *ḥaqīqa* who did not observe the *sharīʿa*, and no Sufi, no matter how elevated his spiritual station, could be exempt from the obligations of the *sharīʿa*.[12]

Another characteristic is the abstruse, esoteric nature of the Sufi sayings. Couched in a vocabulary derived from the Quran and other traditional sources, Sufi pronouncements could be interpreted at different levels. The mystical doctrine was to be taught only to the initiate and only according to the degree of his preparedness;[13] it was not to be divulged to the vulgar.

The expansion of Sufism as a popular movement is connected with the development of Sufi orders. The prominent Sufi orders (Qādiriyya, Suhrawardiyya, Mawlawiyya, Shādhiliyya) which, in one form or another, have survived to the present, appeared only in the sixth and seventh centuries A.H. However, the phenomenon of Sufi brotherhoods and congregations is considerably older, as it looms large in the Sufi compendiums of the fourth and fifth centuries, and it seems to go back originally to the early days of Islamic pietism and mysticism.

In Islam, religious life is conceived within a congregation. This attitude is manifested in the prescription of congregational prayer on Friday as well as in the special merit generally

[11]Qushayrī, *Al-Risāla al-Qushayriyya* (Cairo: Muṣṭafā al-Bābī al-Ḥalabī, 1379/1959), p. 9.

[12]See sec. 21 below.

[13]See secs. 39, 54 below.

attributed to communal prayer. It is quite understandable that Muslim ascetics and mystics preferred to congregate in order to worship together with people who shared their religious tendency. Solitude—although it is regarded by Sufis as one of the means of self-mortification and moral discipline—is not held to be permanently desirable.

Sufi congregations were usually formed around some individual Sufi, famous for his extraordinary spiritual gifts, as aspirants came to be instructed by him. This affiliation of a master (*shaykh*) with his disciple (*murīd*) is the nucleus of all Sufi associations. The communal life of such Sufi groups was centered in the shaykh's residence, which thus became a Sufi convent.

The unmarried members of the Sufi group used to live in the convent, but those who had families would live with their families and come to the convent for the communal activities. Itinerant Sufis, too, would find lodging in such convents.

The members of a Sufi convent would normally perform the obligatory prayers in common and, in addition, would be collectively engaged, under the guidance of the shaykh, in the devotional exercise of remembrance (*dhikr*). In *dhikr* gatherings, selections from the Quran would be recited or chanted, and God's names would be repeated in a certain assigned way. Various shaykhs devised different forms of *dhikr* exercises, each prescribing his particular Quranic selections and preferred formulae of the divine names as well as the fashion in which they had to be said.

In many Sufi groups, *dhikr* assemblies developed into a kind of mystical concert known as *samāʿ* (audition); in these sessions litanies and poems were chanted, and ecstatic dancing often took place.[14]

The shaykh would teach his followers the Sufi doctrine of the mystical way (*ṭarīqa*) and supervise their spiritual progress.

[14]See secs. 27–32, 135–151 below.

It has already been noted that there were some variations in the itinerary of the Sufi way as taught by different masters. The term *ṭarīqa* consequently signifies the way of Sufism in general as well as any one of the prescribed sequences of the stations.

Sufis, whether they be associated with a convent or itinerant, had to accept the rule of poverty (*faqr*), for it is one of the primary stations of the Sufi way. The Sufi, or, more correctly, the aspirant to Sufism, had to renounce his possessions and occupation. In giving up his source of livelihood, the Sufi showed his total trust in God (*tawakkul*, which is another one of the stations). The term *faqīr* or *darwīsh* (meaning "a poor man" or "mendicant" in Arabic and Persian, respectively) is in fact a most common designation for an ordinary Sufi (though not for a Sufi shaykh).[15]

To be sure, many were attracted to Sufism who did not accept the rule of poverty to become *fuqarā'* (plural of *faqīr*). It was customary for such persons to associate themselves with a convent whose shaykh they admired. They would materially support the convent with donations and be allowed to attend *dhikr* ceremonies held there. They were, so to speak, "lay members" of the Sufi brotherhood.[16]

Initially, Sufi brotherhoods were, by and large, local organizations. When a disciple of a shaykh had attained to the station of consummate Sufi, his master could give him permission to instruct others in Sufism. He might then become a shaykh in his own right and possibly form another Sufi brotherhood. Many Sufi convents were thus affiliated through the link of a common original discipleship, but they did not constitute together one universal order. This ramification of independent Sufi brotherhoods is characteristic of the expansion of Sufism until the end of the sixth century A.H.

[15]See sec. 147 below.
[16]Cf. pp. 18–19 below.

From the end of the sixth century, the affiliation of kindred Sufi groups tends to become formalized, in the framework of all-embracing Sufi orders, by attachment to the particular way (*ṭarīqa*) prescribed by the common master. Groups which are thus affiliated practice the same *dhikr* exercises and follow the same system of mystical initiation. In this manner, the term *ṭarīqa* comes to signify "a Sufi order."

The Suhrawardi way (*al-ṭarīqa al-suhrawardiyya*), founded by Abū al-Najīb al-Suhrawardī and by his nephew and disciple Abū Ḥafṣ, appears to be the oldest of these universal Sufi orders. As originator of the Suhrawardiyya and its many suborders, Abū al-Najīb played an important role in the development of popular Sufism.[17]

Abū al-Najīb al-Suhrawardī—A Biographical Note[18]

Abū al-Najīb ʿAbd al-Qāhir b. ʿAbdallāh al-Suhrawardī was born about 490 A.H. (1097 A.D.)[19] in Suhraward, a town in the Jibāl province in the vicinity of Zanjān, in the north-

[17]See *EI Supp.*, s.v. "Ṭarīḳa." Abū al-Najīb's name also appears in the chain of spiritual lineage (*silsila*) of the Mawlawiyya order, and he is regarded by the Shādhiliyya as the originator of their *ṭarīqa*. See H. J. Kissling, "Aus der Geschichte des Chalvetijje Ordens," *Zeitschrift der Deutschen Morgenländischen Gesellschaft*, 103 (1953), Table 1 (opp. p. 282).

[18]See Carl Brockelmann, *Geschichte der Arabischen Literatur*, 2 vols., 2nd ed. (Leiden: E. J. Brill, 1943–1949), I, 436, and his *Geschichte der Arabischen Literatur*, 3 supplementary vols. (Leiden: A. J. Brill, 1937–1949), I, 780. Henceforth cited *GAL* and *GAL Supp.* Both *GAL* and *EI* have only short and rather incomplete biographical notes on Abū al-Najīb. I have derived the data for the biographical note mainly from the following authors: Samʿānī (d. 562/1167), Ibn al-Jawzī (d. 597/1200), Yāqūt (d. 629/1229), Ibn Khallikān (d. 681/1282), Dhahabī (d. 748/1348), Yāfiʿī (d. 768/1367), Subkī (d. 771/1370), and Ibn al-ʿImād (d. 1089/1679). Full details on these sources are given in the bibliography below. The relative value of these sources for Abū al-Najīb's biography, the interdependence of some of them, and the dependence of some on other earlier sources is discussed in the introduction to my edition of the Arabic text. (Forthcoming.)

[19]Samʿānī quotes Abū al-Najīb as saying that he was born *about* 490 A.H.; Ibn Jawzī, *Muntaẓam*, X, 146, also quotes Abū al-Najīb to that effect (probably

western part of Persia. He is said to have been a descendant of the Caliph Abū Bakr.[20] A paternal uncle of Abū al-Najīb, 'Umar b. Muḥammad (d. 532 A.H.), was a Sufi and the head of a convent in Baghdad called *Sa'ādat al-Khādim.*[21] When Abū al-Najīb became a Sufi, he was invested with the Sufi habit by this uncle.[22]

Although there is no information concerning Abū al-Najīb's life and education in his birthplace, it may be assumed that he received traditional training in Quran and Ḥadīth. According to Ibn 'Asākir (quoted in Dhahabī) and Yāqūt, Abū al-Najīb learned Ḥadīth in Isfahan from Abū 'Alī al-Ḥaddād who was a leading traditionist in that city. From this it can be inferred that as a boy in his teens he went to Isfahan, which was the major city of the Jibāl province and a center of learning.[23] Dhahabī and Subkī mention three others under whom Abū al-Najīb studied Ḥadīth: Zāhir b. Ṭāhir, the Qāḍī Abū Bakr al-Anṣārī, and Abū 'Alī b. Nabhān, who was the leading authority on Ḥadīth in Iraq. Abū al-Najīb's studies under Ibn Nabhān must have taken place after Abū al-Najīb had come to Baghdad. According to one source his arrival in Baghdad was in 507 A.H., when he was about

on the basis of Sam'ānī). Ibn Kahllikān gives the year 490 as the year of his birth on the basis of a statement by Abū al-Najīb's nephew, Abū Ḥafṣ. Subkī fixes the date of his birth in 490 in the month of *Ṣafar*.

[20]Sam'ānī and Ibn Khallikān each give genealogies which list twelve generations between Abū al-Najīb and Abū Bakr.

[21]Ibn Jawzī, *Muntaẓam*, X, 75.

[22]See Ibn Baṭṭūṭa, *Riḥlat Ibn Baṭṭūṭā* (Beirut: Dār Ṣādir, 1960), p. 201; Eng. trans. *The Travels of Ibn Baṭṭūṭā*, trans. H. A. R. Gibb, vol. II (Cambridge: Cambridge University Press, 1962), p. 297. Cf. Sha'rānī, *Al-Anwār al-Qudsiyya fī Ma'rifat Qawā'id al-Ṣūfiyya*, 2 vols. (Cairo: al-Maktaba al-'Ilmiyya, 1962), I, pp. 31, 50.

[23]Niẓām al-Mulk, the great Seljuk vizier, founded in Isfahan a *madrasa*, which was named after him *Niẓāmiyya* like its more famous namesake in Baghdad; see George Makdisi, "Muslim Institutions of Learning in Eleventh Century Baghdad," *Bulletin of the School of Oriental and African Studies*, 24 (1961), 44.

seventeen years old.[24] Having achieved a certain proficiency in Ḥadīth, Abū al-Najīb studied jurisprudence (*fiqh*) in the Niẓāmiyya under Asʿad al-Mīhanī. These studies must have been between 507 and 513 A.H.[25] He completed Mīhanī's course in *fiqh*. In Baghdad, Abū al-Najīb also learned Arabic grammar and belles-lettres (*adab*) from al-Faṣīḥī.[26]

When Abū al-Najīb was about twenty-five, he left his academic pursuits to lead a life of solitude and wandering. He subsequently returned to Isfahan to join the company of Aḥmad al-Ghazālī, who became his mentor in Sufism.[27] He ranked there as an esteemed and trustworthy disciple of Ghazālī. There is an account of an instance in which Abū al-Najīb was entrusted by Ghazālī to instruct a new postulant.[28] Abū al-Najīb eventually returned to Baghdad, where he also became a disciple of Ḥammād al-Dabbās (d. 525),[29]

[24]The date 507 A.H. is given by Dhahabī. The other sources do not give the year of his arrival in Baghdad; Subkī says only that he came to Baghdad as a young man. However, the date of 507 for his arrival in Baghdad fits well with other data: Ibn Nabhān, from whom Abū al-Najīb learned Ḥadīth, died in Baghdad in Shawwāl in 511; we are also told that for a whole year before his death he was ill and unconscious.

[25]Asʿad al-Mīhanī (d. 523 A.H.) was thrice appointed to teach *fiqh* in the Niẓāmiyya *madrasa* (see Makdisi, "Muslim Institutions," pp. 41–43). The first time he taught was from 507 to 513. The second time he was appointed was in 517. This was a time of disturbance in the Niẓāmiyya, and it is not clear for how long, if at all, Mīhanī actually taught there. His third appointment was sometime between 521 and 523. Since Abū al-Najīb withdrew from his academic activities before 520 to become a disciple of Aḥmad al-Ghazālī, it must be concluded that he studied with Mīhanī in the period of the latter's first appointment (507–513).

[26]Abū al-Ḥasan ʿAlī b. Muḥammad al-Faṣīḥī had taught grammar in the Niẓāmiyya for some time, but he was accused of Shīʿite leaning and was dismissed. He died in 516. See Yāqūt, *Muʿjam al-Udabāʾ*, 20 vols. in 10 (Cairo: Dār al Maʾmūn, 1936–1938), XV, 66.

[27]Aḥmad al-Ghazālī died in 520 A.H., hence the events mentioned here must have occurred before this year.

[28]See Abū Ḥafṣ Suhrawardī, *ʿAwārif al-Maʿārif* (Beirut: Dār al-Kitāb al-ʿArabī, 1966), p. 68.

[29]Ḥammād al-Dabbās was also the shaykh of ʿAbd al-Qādir al-Jīlanī, the other great Sufi authority in Baghdad, who was the contemporary of Abū al-Najīb.

who was a Sufi shaykh quite different from Aḥmad al-Ghazālī and from Abū al-Najīb himself in that he was not one of the *ʿulamāʾ* class and was even said to have been illiterate. For a number of years, he preferred to live a solitary life of asceticism and self-mortification, earning his living as a water-carrier. After some years of solitude, he began to preach Sufism and to hold *dhikr* assemblies, attracting many followers and novices.[30] He founded a convent (*ribāṭ*) on the western bank of the Tigris, on the site of a ruin in which he had lived, and near the *ribāṭ* he built a *madrasa*. He achieved renown both as an authority in *fiqh*[31] and as a Sufi shaykh. Persons escaping from the wrath of the Sultan or the Caliph sought and found refuge in his convent. According to one source, a number of convents were built in Baghdad for his disciples.

On 27 Muḥarram 545 A.H., Abū al-Najīb was appointed to teach *fiqh* in the Niẓāmiyya.[32] This was the most prestigious academic position a Shāfiʿite scholar could reach. He was dismissed from this office in the month of Rajab 547, and his removal should be seen within the context of the contemporary political scene: the contest for power in Baghdad between the Caliph and the Seljuq Sultan or his representative, the *shiḥna*. The Niẓāmiyya was, so to speak, a Seljuqid institution; its founder, Niẓām al-Mulk, had stipulated that the appointment of the professors of *fiqh* should be a prerogative of him and of his successors.[33] The Caliph al-Muqtafī

[30]Section 40 of Abū al-Najīb's *Kitāb Ādāb al-Murīdīn* teaches that when the Sufi has attained to a high level of Sufi truth, he may return to society and become active in it; at such a stage, his mingling with other people would not have an adverse effect on him. This section perhaps reflects the author's own experience.

[31]Ibn al-Jawzī, *Muntaẓam*, X, 68, records that in 531 A.H. Abū al-Najīb gave public lectures on *fiqh* which were attended by jurists and Qāḍīs.

[32]The date of the appointment is given by Ibn Khallikān and Ibn al-Jawzī, *Muntaẓam*, X, 142.

[33]See Asad Talas, *L'Enseignement chez les Arabes: La Madrasa Nizamiyya et son histoire* (Paris: P. Geuthner, 1939) pp. 34–35; Makdisi, "Muslim Institutions," pp. 46, 50, 55.

also tried to exercise some authority over the affairs of the Niẓāmiyya. Formally he could exercise such authority by refusing to give a new professor of *fiqh* permission to begin his teaching. In his efforts to regain actual power in Baghdad at the expense of the Seljuqid military commander (*shiḥna*), the Caliph al-Muqtafī was aided by his talented and energetic vizier, the Ḥanbalite Ibn Hubayra.[34] It may be gathered that the *fuqahā'* (*fiqh* scholars) of the Niẓāmiyya were opposed to the Caliph's attempts to control the institution. Although Abū al-Najīb had received the Caliph's consent to assume his office at the Niẓāmiyya, he did not have the Caliph's favor and had to rely on the protection of the *shiḥna*. When the Sultan Masʿūd died, the Caliph succeeded in regaining complete power in Baghdad, and the *shiḥna* (Masʿūd Bilāl) had to flee from the city. The Caliph then dismissed Abū al-Najīb from his office and appointed to it a man of his choice.

In his account of the year 547 A.H., Ibn al-Jawzī records some of the events related to Abū al-Najīb's dismissal. Some functionaries of the Caliph's administration came to the Niẓāmiyya to take possession of the estate of a certain deceased person. (These were special officials whose function was to appropriate for the treasury the estates of deceased persons who had no inheritors.) Some *fuqahā'* prevented them from carrying out their task and, in turn, appropriated the possessions for themselves. As a result, two *fuqahā'* were arrested and imprisoned as thieves, by order of the Caliph's court. Consequently, the *fuqahā'* of the Niẓāmiyya declared a strike and publicly demonstrated and protested against the Caliph's administration. The next day, Abū al-Najīb apologized to the Caliph, but, nonetheless, the Caliph suspended him from his teaching. However, under the protection of the

[34]See *EI*², s.v. "Ibn Hubayra"; on the contest of power between Muqtafī and the Sultan, see A. H. Siddiqi, *Caliphate and Sultanate* (Karachi: Jamiyat-ul-Falah, 1963), pp. 184–185.

shiḥna, Abū al-Najīb resumed his teaching in the Niẓāmiyya, in defiance of the Caliph. A few days later, when the *shiḥna* fled from Baghdad, Abū al-Najīb was finally dismissed.[35]

It may be assumed that both before and after his appointment at the Niẓāmiyya, Abū al-Najīb taught *fiqh* and Ḥadīth in his own *madrasa*.[36] He was considered an authoritative *muftī*. In addition to teaching *fiqh* and Ḥadīth, Abū al-Najīb was, of course, engaged in teaching the Sufi doctrine. According to a manuscript note, he had already taught his *Kitāb Ādāb al-Murīdīn* by 550 A.H.[37] We learn from a note on a manuscript of Sarrāj's *Kitāb al-Luma'* that in 553 Abū al-Najīb conducted a course using this book as text.[38]

In 557 A.H., Abū al-Najīb left Baghdad, intending to go on pilgrimage to Jerusalem, but he was unable to continue his journey beyond Damascus because the two-year armistice between Nūr al-Dīn Zenkī and Baldwin had expired.[39] Nūr al-Dīn Zenkī received Abū al-Najīb with great honor in Damascus, where, according to one source, he arrived in 558. During his stay in Damascus, he taught Ḥadīth and held assemblies of *dhikr* and exhortation. After a short period he returned to Baghdad.

He died on Friday, 17 Jumādā II, 563 A.H. (29 March,

[35]See Ibn al-Jawzī, *Muntaẓam*, X, 146–147, and cf. Ibn al-Athīr, XI, 161–162. Sibṭ Ibn al-Jawzī (d. 654–1256), *Mir'āt al-Zamān*, p. 129, relates that after the death of Sultan Mas'ūd, the Caliph arrested a number of people who had been publicly deprecating the rights of the Caliph; he mentions two persons by name, one of whom is Abū al-Najīb. We are also told by Ibn al-Jawzī that in the same week of Abū al-Najīb's dismissal, one of his disciples was accused of Shī'ite leaning and was imprisoned and punished.

[36]The sources list a number of persons who transmitted Ḥadīth on his authority, among them the famous traditionists Sam'ānī and Ibn 'Asākir.

[37]See the description of MS. 'Ayn$_2$, "The Description of the Manuscripts," appended to my Arabic edition of *Kitāb Ādāb al-Murīdīn* (forthcoming).

[38]Sarraj, *Kitāb al-Luma' fī al-Taṣawwuf*, ed. R. A. Nicholson (Leiden: E. J. Brill, and London: Luzac & Co., 1914), p. xxxix.

[39]See K. M. Setton and M. W. Baldwin, eds., *A History of the Crusades* (Philadelphia: University of Pennsylvania Press, 1958), I, 523.

1168 A.D.) at the time of the evening prayer and was buried the next morning in his convent in Baghdad.

Abū al-Najīb was not a prolific writer. In addition to *Kitāb Ādāb al-Murīdīn*, Brockelmann mentions only one book by him, *Gharīb al-Maṣābīḥ*, which was a commentary on *Maṣābīḥ al-Sunna*, the popular Ḥadīth collection of Abū Muḥammad al-Ḥusayn al-Baghawī.[40] Dhahabī (quoting Ibn al-Najjār) says that Abū al-Najīb wrote books, but he does not mention any titles.[41] It is quite curious that none of the above-quoted historical sources mentions *Kitāb Ādāb al-Murīdīn*; the book apparently became widely known only with the spread of the Suhrawardi order after the death of the author.[42] Abū al-Najīb was famous not for his writings but for his activities as a teacher, exhorter, and the founder of a convent; the composition of *Kitāb Ādāb al-Murīdīn* was, in a way, an extension of these activities.

Kitāb Ādāb al-Murīdīn—A Sufi Rule

Kitāb Ādāb al-Murīdīn is unique among Sufi compositions known today in that Sufism in its entirety is viewed here from the standpoint of *ādāb* (rules of conduct).[43] However, a full exposition of Sufi mystical theory is not included in it. One reason for this omission may lie in the fact that the system of

[40]See *GAL Supp.*, I, 620.

[41]Subkī and Yāfiʿi make a similar statement (probably also derived from Ibn al-Najjār). Brockelmann mentions another composition ascribed to Abū al-Najīb, *Sharḥ al-Asmāʾ al-Ḥusnā*, but this is considered to be a pseudepigraph. He was also mentioned as the author of a collection of biographies which has been lost; see George Makdisi, *Ibn ʿAqīl et la résurgence de l'Islam traditionaliste au XIe siècle* (Damascus: Institut Français de Damas, 1963), p. 50.

[42]The later Sufi writer Jāmī (d. 817/1492) mentions this book and quotes a long paragraph from it: almost all of sec. 16 of my Arabic edition; (Jāmī, *Nafaḥāt al-Uns* [Teheran, 1336/1957], p. 417).

[43]See F. Meier, "Ein Knigge für Sufi's," *Revista degli Studi Orientali*, 32 (1957), 489.

stations and states (*maqāmāt* and *aḥwāl*) had already been explained by famous Sufi authors in the two centuries preceding Abū al-Najīb.[44] A more important reason is that the mystical theory and, in particular, the matter of mystical states (*aḥwāl*) constituted the inner aspect of Sufism, whereas novices, for whom the book was primarily intended, were expected to become versed in the external aspect as a first step.[45] This is presumably why, except for a brief summary on the stations and states,[46] Abū al-Najīb deals with the stations only insofar as the matter was required for novices.

The book is characterized by a realistic approach to social necessities and to the moral capabilities of human nature. Abū al-Najīb believed that the Sufi's sphere of activity is within society.[47] He preached that it is better to compromise some of the ideal principles in order to help others in society than to preserve pure principles by isolating oneself from society and caring only for one's own salvation.[48] Therefore, Abū al-Najīb presents an ethical doctrine that is applicable to social reality. The fourth part of the book, in particular, is designed to deal realistically with various common practices which did not conform to the strict rules of conduct required by Sufi theory. For this purpose, the author makes use of the traditional concept of *rukhṣa* ("an ethical dispensation" or "a relaxation of the strict rule") which he applies, however, in a rather new way.[49]

In the concluding chapter of his book, the author says that the category of *rukhaṣ* is the lowest level of attainment in Sufism

[44]Esp., Sarrāj, Kalābādhī, Makkī, and Qushayrī.

[45]See sections 39-41 below.

[46]Sections 49-50 below.

[47]See section 76 below.

[48]See section 89 below.

[49]The opposite of *rukhṣa* (pl. *rukhaṣ*) is *'azīma* (meaning "the strict requirement"); see Massignon, *Passion*, II, 709, n.l.

and that it is especially intended for people whom he designates by the term "simulators" (*mutashabbihūn*) that is, people who try to resemble the Sufis. According to Abū al-Najīb, this term is not derogatory, for he holds that these simulators are truly associated with Sufism. To support this opinion, Abū al-Najīb quotes the saying of the Prophet, "Whoever makes an effort to resemble a group of people is one of them."

Whereas earlier Sufis used the term *mutashabbihūn* pejoratively to signify "those who falsely pretend to be Sufis,"[50] Abū al-Najīb uses it to designate the "lay members" of the Sufi brotherhood.[51] We learn more about the attitude of Abū al-Najīb toward the lay members through his nephew Abū Ḥafṣ al-Suhrawardī, who devotes a special chapter in his *'Awārif al-Ma'ārif* to the question of the *mutashabbihūn* and quotes therein his uncle. In this chapter, Abū al-Najīb is reported to have cited the following Ḥadīth with regard to the *mutashabbihūn*: "Man is [associated] with him whom he loves." He goes on to explain that the *mutashabbihūn* choose to resemble the Sufis because of their love for them and that, although they do not undertake to fulfil all the obligations incumbent upon the regular Sufis, they are one with them through their aspiration.[52] By stressing that it is by virtue of their aspiration (*irāda*) that the lay members are attached to Sufism, Abū al-Najīb seems to suggest that in this respect they are similar to regular novices—*murīdūn*, a term which literally means "aspirants." He states that the *mutashabbihūn* are characterized by their love (*maḥabba*) for Sufism; indeed, in some instances

[50]See Sarrāj, p. 2, l. 18, and p. 3, l. 15; notice also the derogatory connotation of the term in a saying of Sahl al-Tustarī, sec. 47 below.

[51]Since the thirteenth century, this kind of affiliation to Sufism has become the most common form of religious association in Islam. See Hamilton A. R. Gibb and Harold Bowen, *Islamic Society and the West*, vol. I, pt. II (London: Oxford University Press, 1957), p. 185; and also Gibb, *Studies on the Civilization of Islam*, ed. Stanford J. Shaw and William R. Polk (Boston: Beacon Press, 1962), p. 29; Gibb, *Mohammedanism*, pp. 152–153.

[52]See Abū Ḥafṣ Suhrawardī, *'Awārif*, p. 65.

the lay members are referred to as *muḥibbūn* "those who are possessed with love."[53]

Although the affiliation of lay members to Sufism was a phenomenon both very common and of great consequence to the Sufi orders, this subject is hardly discussed in the Sufi manuals. Abū al-Najīb seems to have been the first Sufi author to deal explicitly with this form of association with Sufism and to propose a doctrine of Sufi ethics that would accommodate it. To this effect, Abū al-Najīb uses, as was noted above, the concept of *rukhṣa*. In the Ḥadīth literature, the term *rukhṣa* is applied to deviations from the strict rule in matters of ritual, such as fasting or prayer, which are allowed in such special circumstances as during illness or long trips.[54] The term *rukhṣa* is used in this way with regard to matters of ritual in Ghazālī's *Iḥyā'* and in Jīlānī's *Ghunya*. Ghazālī also applied the term *rukhṣa* to the relaxation, under the pressure of circumstances, of certain ethical requirements.[55] Some Sufi writers utilized the concept of *rukhṣa* to justify the admission of specific Sufi practices, such as the Sufi audition (*samā'*) and the mystical dance, which did not constitute part of the established custom (*sunna*) of Islam.[56]

Notwithstanding such applications of the term *rukhṣa* as an acceptable category in law and ethics, in the Sufi sources there are expressions of objection to *rukhaṣ* and condemnation of those who practice them. It seems that certain Sufis or would-be Sufis availed themselves of the concept of *rukhṣa* and applied it in a rather arbitrary way. Some leading Sufis were therefore moved to voice their opposition to such a practice

[53]See section 151 below and cf. section 109; cf. also the opinion of Aḥmad al-Ghazālī on this matter in James Robson, ed. and trans., *Tracts on Listening to Music* (London: Royal Asiatic Society, 1938), p. 126.

[54]A. J. Wensinck et al., *Concordance et indices de la tradition musulmane* (Leiden: Brill, 1936–), s.v. "*rukhṣa*" and "*rakhkhaṣa*."

[55]For instance, he permits, by way of *rukhṣa*, visiting an impious Sultan in an attempt to prevent some act of injustice.

[56]Cf. Massignon, *Passion*, II, 779.

and thereby to safeguard the orthodoxy of Sufism and its moral reputation. Characterizing the Sufis, Sarrāj says, "It is not their way to practice *rukhaṣ* or to seek [esoteric] interpretations (*ta'wīlāt*).[57]

In a sentence which is clearly derived from the above-cited passage of Sarrāj, Abū al-Najīb says of the Sufis, "It is not their way to seek [esoteric] interpretations,"[58] omitting the phrase about *rukhaṣ*. This omission is deliberate and significant for, as we have seen, Abū al-Najīb made the *rukhaṣ* an integral part of his system of ethics, albeit its lowest level.

The *rukhaṣ* of Abu al-Najīb are intended primarily to make allowance for practices which deviate from the Sufi ethical ideal.[59] Even though the author designates the *rukhaṣ* as suitable only for lay members,[60] it seems that most of these "relaxations of thc strict rule" reflect customs and practices which were common among regular Sufis as well.[61] According to Abū al-Najīb, the *rukhaṣ* may be used only under the constraint of necessity, and he defines for each *rukhṣa* the conditions which would justify its application. In this manner, Abū al-Najīb attempts to preserve ideal principles, while presenting a doctrine of practical ethics.

The great importance which the author himself attached to his doctrine of *rukhaṣ* is quite evident; it is further underlined by the fact that the chapter on *rukhaṣ* contains forty such items, forty being a favorite number with Arab authors. It should be noted that although *Kitāb Ādāb al-Murīdīn* is intended

[57]Sarrāj, p. 10, l. 14. By *ta'wīlāt* he means interpretations intended to justify their deviating opinions or practices.

[58]Section 36 below.

[59]Abū al-Najīb's *rukhaṣ* are not intended to justify Sufi practices which deviate from the non-Sufi orthodox custom. It is significant that Sufi *samā'*, justified by earlier Sufi authors as a *rukhṣa* (cf. above n. 56), is included by him among the standard rules, not among the *rukhaṣ*.

[60]Section 207 below.

[61]The first two *rukhaṣ* are proposed to answer the particular problems of lay members (secs. 167, 168 below).

primarily for novices, it presents, in fact, an ethical doctrine for Sufis in general.

M. J. Kister has demonstrated that a good part of the literary materials of the Sufi *ādāb* literature was derived from the early *adab*.[62] However, the secular elements still contained in the former were submerged by the Ḥadīth material, because the Prophet had come to be regarded by pious Muslims as the model for right behavior in every respect.[63]

There are notable relations between various parts of *Kitāb Ādāb al-Murīdīn* and earlier Sufi works. The statement of the creed (sections 3-15) has close verbal similarity to the parallel articles of the creed in Kalābādhī's *Taʿarruf*. Abū al-Najīb's creed is considerably more concise than that of Kalābādhī, and the two creeds differ somewhat in the order of the articles. More significant is the difference arising from the fact that the two authors belonged to different schools of theology; Abū al-Najīb was an Ashʿarite, whereas Kalābādhī was a Ḥanafite and, as was the custom of this school, accepted the formulation of dogma according to Māturīdī.[64] This difference is manifested, for instance, in their attitude toward the use of the "conditional expression" (*istithnā'*) in the declaration "I am really a Believer if Allah will it" (section 14); Abū al-Najīb, in accordance with the Ashʿarite dogma, approves of the use of *istithnā'*, whereas Kalābādhī, following the Ḥanafite-Māturīdite doctrine, does not include such an article.[65]

[62]See Sulamī, *Kitāb Ādāb al-Ṣuḥba*, ed. M. J. Kister (Jerusalem: Israel Oriental Society, 1954), English introduction, pp. 6–7, and cf. the numerous parallels adduced by Kister in his apparatus.

[63]See Meier, "Ein Knigge für Sufi's," pp. 489–490.

[64]See A. J. Arberry, trans., *The Doctrine of the Ṣūfis* (Cambridge: Cambridge University Press, 1935), p. xi.

[65]On this point of difference between the schools of Ashʿarī and Māturīdī, see A. J. Wensinck, *The Muslim Creed* (Cambridge: Cambridge University Press, 1932), pp. 138–139, and Shaykh-Zādeh, *Naẓm al-Farā'id wa-Jamʿ al-Fawā'id* (Cairo, n.d.), pp. 64–65. See other such points of difference in sections 11 and 19 below.

It appears that Abū al-Najīb did not hesitate to draw upon the statement of the creed in Kalābādhi's *Ta'arruf*, even though its author belonged to a different school, as long as the formulations were in agreement with the doctrine of his own school; but in matters which were subject to dispute between the school of Ash'arī and the school of Māturīdī, Abū al-Najīb was, of course, loyal to the Ash'arite doctrine.

When *Kitāb Ādāb al-Murīdīn* is compared with Ghazālī's *Iḥyā'*, it will be discovered that most of the ethical rules contained in parts III and IV of the former book may be found in one form or another in the *Iḥyā'* (particularly in the *Rub' al-'Ādāt*). In the same way, similarities may be found between *Kitāb Ādāb al-Murīdīn* and Jīlānī's *Ghunya* and Makkī's *Qūt al-Qulūb*. However, since these rules and customs were the common stock of Muslim writers, the similarities should not suggest that Abū al-Najīb depends literarily on any of the above-mentioned books in particular. Most of the Sufi anecdotes and sayings in the book are also found in Qushayrī's *Risāla* or Sulamī's *Ṭabaqāt*. These materials, by their very nature, belong to the Sufi common stock. So here again the occurrence of similarities cannot in itself prove literary dependence, although it may be assumed that Abū al-Najīb was indeed familiar with both the *Risāla* and Sulamī's *Ṭabaqāt*.

Abū al-Najīb's chapter on companionship (sections 76–102) appears to be related to Sulamī's *Ādāb al-Ṣuḥba*. Here there is similarity not merely in individual sayings and rules but also in the organization of the material. The numerous parallels between Abū al-Najīb's book and Sulamī's *Jawāmi' Ādāb al-Ṣūfiyya* and his *'Uyūb al-Nafs* seem to indicate that Abū al-Najīb was familiar with these works and drew upon them.

Kitāb Ādāb al-Murīdīn is closely related to *Kitāb al-Luma'* of Sarrāj. The similarities between these two works appear not only in what has been termed "the Sufi common stock" (anecdotes and sayings) but also in other points.[66] As there is evidence that Abū al-Najīb taught *Kitāb al-Luma'*,[67] one may safely conclude that the similarities between this book and *Kitāb Ādāb al-Murīdīn* are due to the direct influence of Sarrāj's book on Abū al-Najīb.

Most of the Ḥadīths quoted in *Kitāb Ādāb al-Murīdīn* can be found in the various known Ḥadīth collections or biographies of the Prophet; I have not made note of such parallels. However, it is of some interest to point out, in the apparatus of my Arabic text, the parallels found in Baghawī's Ḥadīth collection, *Maṣābīḥ al-Sunna*, on which Abū al-Najīb had written a commentary.

Kitāb Ādāb al-Murīdīn is a book steeped in the Sufi literary tradition and containing materials from various sources; however, all the variegated elements were recast by the author in his own mold.

The language of the author is clear and simple, unmarred by affected rhymed prose.[68] In his statement of the creed, the author does not use dialectic-scholastic argumentation. In quoting Ḥadīths and Sufi sayings, Abū al-Najīb does not adduce the chain of authorities (*isnād*) but gives only the name of the earliest authority or, quite often, introduces the saying simply by "it is said" or "one of them said."

Some elements of older *adab* literature—quite secular in origin—are also included in the book. In this respect it resembles and continues the tradition of Sulamī's *Ādāb al-Ṣuḥba* which, in the words of its editor, "forms a link between the

[66]Note esp. the parallels in sections 34–38, indicated in my edition of the Arabic text.

[67]See p. 15 above and n. 38.

[68]Abū al-Najīb was known for his avoidance of the use of rhyming (*tasjī'*) in his preaching.

Adab and Sufi literature."[69] In Abū al-Najīb's composition, however, the older *adab* elements are fully blended in the Islamic-Sufi mold.

These literary and stylistic features make the book easy to read, which accords with its purpose—to serve as a popular manual.

The popularity of *Kitāb Ādāb al-Murīdīn* appears to have been considerable. The large number of extant manuscripts—we presently know of thirty-five—may be taken as one measure of its popularity. The dates of the manuscripts (from the seventh to the eleventh century A.H.) reflect a continued interest in this book down through the centuries. Copies of the book are found in various places from India to Tunisia; the manuscripts were transcribed in such cities as Medina, Damascus, Jerusalem, and Cairo.[70] A Persian translation of almost the entire *Kitāb Ādāb al-Murīdīn* is incorporated in the Persian manual of Sufism, *Awrād al-Aḥbāb wa-Fuṣūṣ al-Ādāb* of Abū al-Mafākhir Yaḥyā Bākharzī (d. 736 A.H.).[71] A commentary on the book was composed by ʿAlī b. Sulṭān Muḥammad al-Qāri' al-Harawī (d. 1014/1605);[72] a Persian paraphrase was written by Muḥammad b. Yūnus al-Ḥusaynī Gisūderāz (d. 825/1422).[73]

Some passages of the book are included in Abū Ḥafṣ al-Suhrawardī's *ʿAwārif al-Maʿārif*. The book seems also to have been a source for the *Ādāb al-Murīdīn* of Najm al-Dīn al Kubrā (d. 618/1221).[74]

[69]Cf. Sulamī, *Ādāb al-Ṣuḥba*, Eng. intro., pp. 6–7.

[70]See "The Description of the Manuscripts" in my edition of the Arabic text.

[71]It should be noted that Bākharzī's Sufi lineage goes back to Abū al-Najīb al-Suhrawardī; see Bākharzī, *Awrād al-Aḥbāb wa-Fuṣuṣ al-Ādāb* (Teheran: Publications de l'Université Téhéran, 1966), "Introduction," pp. 27–28.

[72]See Brockelmann, *GAL*, II, 394, and H. Ritter, "Philologika IX: Die vier Suhrawardī," *Der Islam*, 25 (1939), 36.

[73]See Brockelmann, *GAL*, II, 394.

[74]Cf. F. Meier, "Ein Knigge für Sufi's." Kubrā's Sufi lineage goes back through

Kitāb Ādāb al-Murīdīn is a relatively short composition. In the manuscripts it is divided into twenty-six chapters (*fuṣūl*) of unequal length, each discussing some particular problem.[75] The book contains four major parts, although it is not formally divided in such a way. The four parts are: I, a statement of fundamental beliefs; II, Sufism as one of the religious sciences; III, Sufi ethics; and IV, special dispensations. For purposes of reference and textual analysis a more detailed division is necessary and I have therefore divided the text into 208 sections.

Section 1 is the conventional blessing on the Prophet and his family.

Section 2 is a brief introduction concerning the purpose of the book.

Part I. Sections 3–15 are a statement of the Islamic creed. Sections 16–32 expound the fundamental Sufi beliefs on poverty, miracles, and Sufi audition (*samāʿ*).

Part II. Sections 32–38 define the place of Sufism in relation to the other religious sciences. Sections 39–44 explain that the Sufis vary in accomplishment and rank: there are novices (*murīdūn*), Sufis of intermediate rank (*mutawassiṭūn*), and "knowers" (*ʿārifūn*). Sufism has external and internal aspects, the internal being clearly a higher stage of attainment (section 41). Each Sufi should strive to achieve that stage which is proper for him: the novice should first become accomplished in the external part of Sufism, which is generally synonymous with the *adab* (ethical conduct). Sections 45–48 praise the ethical qualities. Sections 49–50 list and define briefly the

---

his teacher ʿAmmār al-Bidlīsī to Abū al-Najīb al-Suhrawardī; see Meier, *Die Fawāʾiḥ al-Ǧamāl wa-Fawātiḥ al-Ǧalāl des Naǧm ad-Dīn al-Kubrā* (Wiesbaden: Franz Steiner Verlag, 1957), p. 19.

[75]The chapter (*faṣl*) about ecstatic utterances (at the end of section 57 below) contains only one sentence. It seems that Abū al-Najīb devoted a special *faṣl* to this subject, following the example of Sarrāj's book which has a lengthy chapter on that matter.

Sufi stations and states. Section 51 explains that there are different ways to attain to the Sufi truth and that in each of these ways the novice should have a master to guide him. Sections 52–53 emphasize the value of *ʿilm*, religious learning.

Part III. Section 54 begins a series of chapters on Sufi rules of conduct. Sections 54–60 discuss the problem of the transmission and communication of Sufi knowledge. (The author classifies this material under the heading: "the ethics of conversation.") Sections 61–75: rules for the novice at the early stages; 76–102: the ethics of companionship; 103–104: the rules of visiting and hospitality; 105–113: the rules of traveling; 114–120: the rules of dress; 121–130: the rules of eating; 131–133: the rules of sleep; 135–151: the rules of *samāʿ* (Sufi audition), including a detailed discussion of the custom of throwing off the Sufi mantle (*khirqa*) during the *samāʿ* (148–151); 152–154: the rules of marriage; 155–158: the rules of begging; 159: conduct during illness; 160–162: conduct on the deathbed; 163–165: conduct in times of trial.

Part IV. Sections 166–206: the rules of ethical dispensations; 207: a concluding chapter discussing the various levels of religious and ethical attainment; 208: the author's closing prayer.

The grouping of sections outlined above corresponds in general to the division of chapters by Abū al-Najīb.

The division into four parts and short sections is based on criteria of form as well as contents; in part I, for example, almost all sections begin with the phrase *wa-ajmaʿū ʿalā anna* (and they unanimously agree that) or *wa-anna* (and that). In part IV, every section begins with the word *wa-minhā* (among them is).

Rules for the Novice

Kitāb Ādāb al-Murīdīn

AN ABRIDGED TRANSLATION

1. A blessing on the Prophet and his family.

2. Everyone who seeks a thing should know its essence and true nature so that his desire for it may be fulfilled. No one can properly know the way of the Sufis until he knows their fundamental beliefs, their rules of conduct (*ādāb*),[1] and their technical terms.

Because of the great number of false pretenders, the state of the true Sufis has been ignored. However, the corruption of the former should not impugn the upright.[2]

[1]The word *ādāb* (plural of *adab*) is rendered in this translation as "ethics"or "rules of conduct."

It is difficult to convey the exact connotations of these terms for they have different meanings that are interrelated and partially overlapping. *Ādāb* means rules of conduct and *adab* (sing.) consequently sometimes means proper conduct. In a different context, *adab* or *ādāb* can mean belles-lettres. One could perhaps say that either the singular or the plural form can be rendered approximately as culture in two senses: (a) the contents of a certain culture and (b) the literature intended to transmit this cultural content and to educate. Sections 42 and 43 below offer examples of this interrelationship and overlapping. For further details on these terms, see Meir, "Ein Knigge für Sufi's."

[2]The need to distinguish between genuine Sufis and those who arrogate this title to themselves is a recurrent theme in Sufi works; see parallels in my edition of the Arabic text, sec. 2, a.

PART I

3. God (*allāh*) is one, having no partner, no rival, no equal. He is described by the terms in which He described Himself. He is not a body nor a substance nor an accident. He cannot be encompassed by thought, His reality cannot be truly expressed, and sight cannot perceive Him. Everything said in relation to Him is only by supposition. We do not say "His being (*kawnuhu*)"[3] but rather "His existence" (*wujūduhu*), because not every existent (*mawjūd*) is a [generated] being (*kā'in*), but every generated being is existent. God is unlike anything that can be imagined or understood. The questions when? how? where? cannot be asked with regard to God, for He existed before time; His essence is concealed from description; and He is beyond place. The cause of everything is His creation, but there is no cause to His creation. His essence (*dhāt*) is not like other essences and His attributes (*ṣifāt*) are not like other attributes.

4. All that is mentioned in the Quran and the Ḥadīth concerning the Face, the Hand, the Soul, the Hearing, and the Sight of God is affirmed. The doctrine of the Sufis concerning "God's sitting on the throne" is, in conformity with the dictum of Mālik b. Anas on this matter, that belief in it is obligatory. Such is also their doctrine on the descent of God.

5. The Quran is the uncreated speech of God.

6. The possibility of the beatific vision (*ru'yat allāh*) in paradise by eyesight is affirmed. (Ḥadīth is quoted to prove this.)

7. All the details of eschatology included in the Quran and in the Ḥadīth are affirmed. The list is as follows: paradise, hell, the tablet, the pen, the basin, intercession, the *ṣirāṭ* bridge, the balance, the trumpet, the punishment in the tomb, the interrogation by the angels Munkar and Nakīr, the saving of some people from hell by intercession, the belief that paradise and hell will exist forever and that their inhabitants

[3] *Kawn* is the Arabic equivalent of the philosophical term "generation."

will be in them forever; however, Muslims who have committed grave sins will not be in hell forever.

8. God creates the actions of men, just as He creates men themselves. Also, polytheism and disobedience occur by the judgment and predestination of God. Prayer is permitted behind any *imām*, pious or impious.

9. The office of the Caliph belongs to Quraysh [the tribe of the Prophet]. Revolt is prohibited even if the ruler is unjust.

10. The hierarchy of excellence: prophets are the most excellent of mankind, Muḥammad is the most excellent of prophets, then [after the prophets] come Abū Bakr, ʿUmar, ʿUthmān, and ʿAlī in this order, then the rest of the ten [Companions] about whom Muḥammad testified that they will enter paradise and all others about whom Muḥammad testified, then [the rest of] the generation of the Prophet, then the *ʿulamā'* who observe the law, then those who are the most useful to others.

11. There is unanimous agreement that the Messengers are more excellent than angels,[4] but there is variance as to the order of priority between men and angels.

12. It is a religious duty to seek that which is permitted.[5] Whoever appears to be good should not be suspected with regard to his property and gain.

13. Compete faith (*īmān*)[6] consists of confirmation by the tongue, belief within the heart, and performance of the basic duties of Islam (*al-arkān*). He who does not fulfil the first

[4]This is the opinion of Ashʿarī's school; see on this question Shaykh-Zādeh, p. 68, and cf. Kalābādhi, *Kitāb al-Taʿrruf li-Madhhab Ahl al-Taṣawwuf* (Cairo, 1960), pp. 68-69, or its English translation in Arberry, *Doctrine of the Ṣūfis*, p. 53. Kalābādhī states that it cannot be determined whether the prophets are superior to the angels or vice versa.

[5]This article is rather typical of Abū al-Najīb's approach to ethics in general. It differs quite radically from the more ascetic Sufi attitude—to shun even what is permitted.

[6]The word "faith" is used here as an approximate rendering of *īmān*, which signifies the sum total of attributes that qualify a man as a true Muslim (*mu'min*).

requirement is an unbeliever (*kāfir*); he who does not fulfil the second is a hypocrite (*munāfiq*); he who abandons practice is a sinner (*fāsiq*), and whoever does not follow the custom of the Prophet is an innovator (*mubtadiʿ*).

14. It is considered proper to use the conditional expression (*istithnāʾ*) in regard to the declaration of belief.[7] Ḥasan al-Baṣrī was asked, "Are you truly a *muʾmin* (believer)?" He answered, "If you ask me about that [attribute] by virtue of which I may not be slain with impunity by another Muslim, and what I slaughter is lawfully edible, and I may marry a Muslim woman—then I am truly a believer. If, however, you ask me about that [attribute] by virtue of which I may enter paradise and be saved from hell and gain His pleasure—then I am truly a believer, if Allah will it."[8] (Quran and Ḥadīth are quoted in support of the use of *istithnāʾ*.)

15. It is permitted to occupy oneself in commerce and crafts. The lowest way of earning one's livelihood is begging.

16. Poverty (*faqr*) is better than riches. Gabriel advised the Prophet not to accept the treasures of the earth. (Quotations from Quran and Ḥadīth are adduced to prove the preferability of poverty.)

17. Poverty is not identical with Sufism (*taṣawwuf*); rather, the completion of the former stage is the beginning of the latter. The Sufi is different from the Malāmatī, for the Malāmatī is one who would not demonstrate a good work nor conceal a bad one,[9] whereas the Sufi does not concern himself at all with the opinion that other people have of him.

18. It is preferable not to be occupied with commerce and

[7]See Introduction above and n. 65.

[8]Ḥasan al-Baṣrī is making a distinction here between two aspects of *īmān*: (a) a formal-legal aspect, which is the condition of membership in the community of Islam, and (b) a mysterious mode of being which involves the final bliss. Ḥasan uses the "conditional expression" with respect to the latter aspect of *īmān*.

[9]The Malāmatī attempts to demonstrate in this manner that he is free from ostentation.

crafts but rather to devote oneself to acts of piety; this rule is applicable to such people who, having complete trust in God's providence, are not concerned with worldly matters.

19. They all agree that the acts of men are not the cause of bliss or damnation, because pleasure and wrath (*riḍā* and *sukhṭ*) are eternal attributes of God which are not changed by the acts of men.[10] God causes man to act according to His decree, and men should accept the divine decree with pleasure (*riḍā*).[11]

20. Fear and hope are both necessary to prevent bad conduct.[12]

21. Observance of the laws is necessary. God may remove the sense of burden arising from the legal duties from him whose heart becomes pure[13] but not the obligations themselves, because the human qualities do not cease in anyone. Some classes of men are freed in various degrees from human weaknesses; these are, in declining order: *ṣiddīqūn* (saints), *ʿārifūn* (knowers, or Sufis who have achieved the esoteric knowledge), *murīdūn* (novices).

22. Love for the sake of God (*al-ḥubb fī allāh*) and hate for the sake of God (*al-bughḍ fī allāh*) are among the firmest ties of the faith.[14] It is obligatory, within the limits of capability, to

[10]It is noteworthy that in the corresponding chapter in Kalābādhī's *Taʿarruf* there is no such statement concerning God's wrath and pleasure. The Māturīdites did not agree that God's pleasure and wrath cannot be affected by the acts of man. On this difference between the Ashʿarites and the Maturīdites, see Shaykh-Zādeh, pp. 62–63.

[11]The concept of *riḍā* has two aspects: when used in reference to God, it signifies His benevolence; when used in reference to man, it means acceptance of and contentment with the divine decree.

[12]I.e., fear of punishment and hope for reward in the hereafter.

[13]He "whose heart becomes pure" is undoubtedly the Sufi. This phrase seems to allude to the popular etymology of Sufi from *ṣafā*, i.e., to be pure (cf. Sarrāj, p. 26, and Eng. abstract, p. 9; cf. also Kalābādhī, p. 21, and its Eng. trans., Arberry, *Doctrine of the Ṣūfis*, p. 5).

[14]The expression *fī allāh* used here and elsewhere means that social relations should be motivated not by worldly considerations but by religious motives. See the use of this expression in secs. 103, 106 below.

commend the good and forbid evil (*al-amr bil-maʿrūf wal-nahy ʿan al-munkar*).[15]

23. They all agree in affirming the belief in the miracles of saints. The difference between the miracles of saints (*karāmāt*) and the miracles of prophets (*muʿjizāt*) is that the prophet is required to publish the miracle, whereas the saint should conceal the grace (*karāma*) which God vouchsafed to him, unless God causes it to be publicly known.

24. They disapprove of disputes on matters of theology and recommend that one be occupied in legal and ethical matters.

25. They all agree on the permissibility of wearing all clothes except what is prohibited by the *sharīʿa*, namely, what is made mostly of silk. The Sufis prefer worn clothes and patched frocks (*muraqqaʿāt*), and they choose to wear patched frocks for a number of reasons.

26. The color preferred by the Prophet was green. The Prophet also said, "Your best clothes are white." But this means "your most beautiful clothes and those most suitable for other people."[16]

27. They all agree that it is commendable to recite the Quran in a beautiful voice or melody, as long as this does not violate the meaning.[17]

28. As for listening (in the course of *samāʿ*) to poems and songs [one should apply to it the dictum of the Prophet]: having been asked about poetry, the Prophet said, "It is a kind of speech, some of it is (morally) good and hence com-

[15]Sections 20–22 are linked to section 19; in the Arabic text this is evident, since these sections are syntactically dependent on the introductory phrase of section 19, *wa-ajmaʿū*, "they all agree." Section 19 presents the dogma that all the acts of man are predestined by God. This theological dogma may have disruptive effects on moral attitudes; it is therefore counterbalanced in sections 20–22 by stressing the psychological attitude (fear-hope) and legal and social obligations.

[16]This section is intended to justify the Sufi practice of wearing clothes in special colors, which was considered by some as a deviation from the custom (*sunna*) of the Prophet. See parallels in my edition of the Arabic text.

[17]This section justifies the Sufi practice of mystical audition (*samāʿ*).

mendable, some is repugnant and hence reprehensible." Poetry should therefore be judged on the basis of its subject matter and classified as commendable, permissible, disapproved, or forbidden. He who has divine knowledge may listen to such poems as are disapproved of for other people, because he can distinguish between natural inclination and reprehensible desire, between divine inspiration and satanic temptation.

29. (A number of sayings on the subject of *samāʿ*.)

30. (People who attend the Sufi audition differ as to their state (*ḥāl*) while listening. Some are overcome by fear (*khawf*) or grief (*ḥuzn*) or yearning (*shawq*); it may cause them to weep and groan and tear their clothes and become unconscious. Others are overcome with hope (*rajāʾ*) and joy (*faraḥ*) and delight (*istibshār*), and this may induce them to rejoice and dance and clap their hands.)

31. The *samāʿ* may arouse in the participant a desire for the Beloved, and consequently he will jump and turn about, moved by the spirit (*rūḥ*) desiring to ascend back to its heavenly origin.[18] Or this dance may be performed by the Sufis in order to divert or relieve themselves while in the state of *samāʿ*. The latter practice is not forbidden; however it is not one of the qualities of those who attain to the "reality."

32. Abū ʿAbdallāh al-Rūdhabārī on *samāʿ*: "The secret (*sirr*) of him who is truthful in the *samāʿ* consists of three things: knowledge of God, fulfillment of what is required by his spiritual state, and concentration of religious ambition (*jamʿ al-himma*)."[19] He stipulates three conditions with regard to the place where the *samāʿ* may properly be held. The listeners may be in three inner states: love, fear, and hope

[18]This is an interesting explanation of the mental origin of the mystical dance. See a similar explanation by Aḥmad al-Ghazālī in Robson, *Tracts on Listening to Music*, p. 159 (and Eng. trans., pp. 99–100).

[19]On the significance of *himma*, see F. Meier, *Die Fawāʾiḥ al-Ǧamāl*, pp. 233ff.

(*maḥabba, khawf, rajā'*). Movement in the course of *samā'* may be inspired by three inner states: rapture (*ṭarab*), ecstatic yearning (*wajd*), and fear. Each of these has three characteristic symptoms: rapture—dancing, clapping, and joy; ecstatic yearning—absence of selfhood (*ghayba*),[20] loss of personal will and consciousness (*iṣṭilām*),[21] and screaming; fear—weeping, slapping oneself, and moaning.

PART II

33. With regard to the branches of religion and its ordinances, the Sufis agree that one should learn the ordinances of the *sharī'a* so that praxis (*'amal*) would be in conformity with the teachings of the religious-legal science (*'ilm*).[22] They prefer the school of the traditionist jurists, but they do not disapprove of divergence among the religious scholars (*'ulamā'*) in matters of specific applications.

34. The religious scholars are classified in three groups: traditionists (*aṣḥāb al-ḥadīth*), jurists (*fuqahā'*), and Sufi *'ulamā'*. The traditionists are attached to the external meaning of the Ḥadīth; they are the watchmen of religion.

35. The *fuqahā'*, who have received the knowledge of the traditionists, are distinguished by their understanding of legal matters and their ability to make legal inferences. They are the arbiters of religion and its distinguished authorities.

36. The Sufis are in agreement with the two former classes in their inner modes and their outward behavior. It is not of the Sufi way to seek [arbitrary] esoteric interpretations (*ta'wīlāt*) nor to follow one's desires.

[20]Cf. Hujwīrī, *Kashf al-Maḥjūb*, trans. R. A. Nicholson (Leiden: E. J. Brill, and London; Luzac & Co., 1911), p. 248.

[21]Cf. ibid., p. 390.

[22]The requirement of conformity between practice and theory recurs in the book in various forms. One should notice in this connection the expression "the *'ulamā'* who observe the law," in Arabic: *al-'ulamā' al-'āmilūn*, literally, "the *'ulamā'* who practice [what they teach]" (see sections 10 above and 59 below).

37. The Sufis are distinguished by lofty sciences and noble states (*aḥwāl*), and they discuss the science of mutual relations, the faults of commission and omission, and the noble stations (*maqāmāt*). (Sufi technical terms signifying the various *maqāmāt* and *aḥwāl* are enumerated here by way of example.) They also have concepts which are derived [from the Quran and the Ḥadīth] and which are beyond the understanding of the jurists. (Another list of Sufi terms is presented.) So they are the protectors of religion and its eminent leaders.

38. Whoever has difficulty in understanding one of the three sciences, namely, Ḥadīth, jurisprudence, and Sufism should refer his questions to those who are experts in that particular science. Thus, questions relating to the study of Ḥadīth should be referred to the traditionists, questions on matters of law, to the jurists, and questions concerning ethical scrupulosity and the inner states and stations (*aḥwāl* and *maqāmāt*), to the masters of Sufism.

39. The answers to questions about Sufism vary according to the spiritual station of the enquirer: the novice (*murīd*) is answered with regard to the external aspect of Sufism, that is, concerning mutual relations (ethics). The Sufi of the middle rank (*mutawassiṭ*) is answered with regard to the inner states (*aḥwāl*), and the knower (*ʿārif*) is answered with regard to the reality (*al-ḥaqīqa*). The beginning of Sufism is learning (*ʿilm*), the middle is praxis (*ʿamal*), and the end is grace.

40. Sufis are of three ranks: *murīd*, *mutawassiṭ*, and *muntahin* (he who has arrived at the final stage). The *murīd* is a man of momentary experience (*waqt*), the Sufi of the middle rank has inner spiritual states, and the Sufi of the highest rank is a man of reposeful breathing. The Sufi of the middle rank (*mutawassiṭ*) is in the process of ascending from one state to the next, but the consummate Sufi (*muntahin*) is in a position of stability, and he is immune to the effects of the changeful states of mind or harsh circumstances. Zulaykhā is presented as an example

of one who has reached the position of stability. Zulaykhā, having attained to the position of stability in her love for Joseph, was not affected like her friends at the sight of Joseph.[23] This is also attested to by the example of the Prophet, who at first had practiced solitude but afterwards mingled with people. Likewise, the "people of the portico," when they had reached the state of stability, became commanders and administrators, and mixing with the people did not damage their religious position.[24]

41. This school (Sufism) has external and internal aspects (*ẓāhir* and *bāṭin*). The external aspect is to observe the rule of ethical behavior in relation to mankind, and the inner aspect is to launch into the *aḥwāl* and *maqāmāt* in relation to the Real One (*al-ḥaqq*).

42. When the Prophet saw a man jesting during prayer he said, "If his heart were humble, his limbs too would be submissive." Junayd disapproved of the manners practiced by Abū Ḥafṣ al-Ḥaddād [al-Nīsābūrī] and termed them, ironically, princely manners. To this Abū Ḥafṣ answered, "External *adab* reflects the inner *adab*." It is said that the whole of Sufism is *adab;* each moment (*waqt*),[25] each state, and each station has its *adab*. "*Adab* is the support of the poor and the decor of the rich."

43. People are divided into three classes with regard to *adab*: people of this world, people of religion, and the choicest of the people of religion. The *ādāb* of the people of this world consist of knowledge of language and rhetoric, sciences, history, and poetry.

[23]Zulaykhā is the name of the wife of Joseph's Egyptian master, according to post-Quranic Islamic legends. See *EI*, s.v. "Yūsuf b. Yaʿḳūb."

[24]The "people of the portico," a group of pious companions of the Prophet, were considered by the Sufis as the ideal prototype of Islamic piety; see EI^2, s.v. "Ahl al-Ṣuffa."

[25]*Waqt* in the Sufi technical sense signifies the moment of experience. See Qushayrī, p. 33 and Meier, *Die Fawāʾiḥ al-Ǧamāl*, p. 48.

The *ādāb* of the people of religion are, in addition to religious learning: to discipline oneself, to observe the legal prohibitions, to abstain from morally dubious things, and to hasten to do good works.

The *ādāb* of the choicest of the people of religion consist of preserving the heart and observing the secret (*sirr*)[26] and being the same both secretly and outwardly.

44. The novices vary in rank with regard to praxis, those in the middle position vary with regard to their *adab*, and the knowers, with regard to their spiritual ambition (*himma*). The value of each person is according to his *himma*. (Some sayings on *nafs* (soul) and *himma*.)

45. The most noble characteristics of the Sufis are their moral qualities. ʿĀ'isha said that the ethical nature of the Prophet was the Quran. The Prophet said, "The closest to me on the day of resurrection will be he who is best with regard to ethics." He also said, "Bad moral nature is a sign of ill fortune." A saying of Abū Bakr al-Kattānī: "Sufism is ethical disposition, so whoever is better than you in his ethics is greater than you in Sufism."

46. (A list of some ethical qualities postulated by the Sufis.)

47. When Sahl b. ʿAbdallāh [al-Tustarī] was asked about good ethical behavior, he said that its minimal requirements were to suffer evil with forbearance, to abstain from retribution, and to have compassion for him who wrongs you. It is these qualities which are characteristic of the Sufis and not what is said and committed by the simulators (*mutashabbihūn*); their perverted claims are denounced.[27]

48. Abū Yazīd al-Bisṭāmī saw a man who had made him-

[26]*Sirr* signifies the loftiest element in the spiritual essence of man; the *sirr* is the place of the ultimate mystical experience. See Meier, *Die Fawā'iḥ al-Ǧamāl*, pp. 173ff. and *passim*.

[27]It seems that this denouncement is directed against would-be Malāmatīs who, under the guise of purposely incurring censure, actually sought to satisfy their desires.

self famous for his asceticism (*zuhd*) spitting mucus in the direction of the Qibla. Abū Yazīd said, "He cannot be trusted about a rule of the *sharīʿa*, so how can he be trusted about his claim to sainthood?"

49. The stations (*maqāmāt*). *Maqām* signifies the position of man in worship before God. The stations are: awakening out of carelessness, repentance (*tawba*), returning (*ināba*), moral scrupulosity (*waraʿ*), examination of the soul (*muḥāsabat al-nafs*), aspiration (*irāda*), renunciation (*zuhd*),[28] poverty (*faqr*), veracity (*ṣidq*), and forbearance (*taṣabbur*), which is the last station of novices. Then come patience (*ṣabr*), satisfaction (*riḍā*), total sincerity (*ikhlāṣ*), trust in God (*tawakkul*). (Each of the above stations is defined by one sentence.)

50. The states (*aḥwāl*) and their definition. Junayd defined *ḥāl* as a form of inspiration which comes down to the heart but does not stay in it permanently. A list of the states: attentive observation (*murāqaba*), nearness (*qurb*), love (*maḥabba*), hope (*rajāʾ*), fear (*khawf*), diffidence (*ḥayāʾ*). The last four are considered to result from the state of nearness, because, while in the latter state, some people are overcome by fear and diffidence and others by love and hope. Then come yearning (*shawq*), intimacy (*uns*), serenity (*ṭumaʾnīna*), certainty (*yaqīn*), and the experience of vision (*mushāhada*), which is the last of the states. Then come various forms of divine inspiration: signs (*fawātiḥ*),[29] appearances of light, and graces, all of which are ineffable.

51. The ways vary, but the goal is one. The ways vary because of the variation in the states and stations of those who follow them. Various possible ways are listed: worship, self-discipline, solitude and retirement, wandering and being

[28]In translating the word *zuhd*, one should distinguish between *zuhd* as a general term, signifying the outlook and practice of early Muslim ascetics, and *zuhd* as one particular station in the system of *maqāmāt*. In the former sense it is translated as "asceticism," in the latter as "renunciation."

[29]On the meaning of this term see Meier, *Die Fawāʾiḥ al-Ǧamāl*, p. 50.

remote from one's home, service to the brethren, self-mortification, and engagement in the *aḥwāl*, forfeiture of one's social standing, [recognizing one's] weakness and failure, learning and inquiry. In any one of these ways one should have an instructor and guide in order to be protected from perplexity and temptation.

52. The merit of knowledge (*ʿilm*). (Quran 3:18 is quoted.) In this verse God mentions the people of *ʿilm* next to Himself and the angels. The Prophet said, " *ʿUlamāʾ* are the successors of prophets." He said, "The learned man is superior to the [unlearned] worshiper as I am superior to the least man among you." He also said, "Men are of two kinds: the learned and those who strive to acquire learning, and the rest are riffraff." It is also said, " *ʿIlm* is the root and *ʿamal*—the branch."

53. The majority of the Sufi masters consider *ʿilm* to be superior to both *maʿrifa* (gnosis) and *ʿaql* (intellect or reason), because Allah has the attribute of *ʿilm* and because *ʿilm* has dominance over reason and not vice versa. (An argument to prove the preeminence of *ʿilm* is drawn from the story of King Solomon and the hoopoe, and Quran 27:22 is quoted.)

PART III

54. Sufi ethics in conversation (*muḥāwara*).[30] Their purpose in conversation should be to offer advice and guidance and whatever can benefit other people. The Sufi should speak to people according to their intellectual capacity. (A saying of the Prophet on the latter point.) The novice should not speak on any question unless he is asked about it, and his answer should be suited to [the understanding of] the interrogator. (A saying of Junayd on this subject.)

55. The novice should ask only questions pertaining to his

[30]Under the heading of this term, Suhrawardī deals with matters concerning the teaching and discussion of Sufi doctrine.

station. He should not speak about what he has not practiced, but some say that it is permissible. (A saying of the Prophet in support of the latter view.) Knowledge should be divulged only to qualified persons, although another view has it that it may be divulged to others as well. One should not speak in front of a more learned man.

56. One should not seek to obtain social standing or worldly goods through his knowledge. Two traditions of the Prophet on the above subject. One should strive to practice what he hears and learns. "Whoever hears something of the Sufi doctrine (*ʿulūm al-qawm*) and practices it, it becomes wisdom in his heart, and those who listen to him will derive benefit from it; but whoever hears and does not practice, it is mere talk which he will forget after a few days." It is said: "If words come out of the heart they will enter the heart, but if they come from the tongue they will not pass beyond the ears."

57. The merit of speech and silence on different occasions. Junayd and Ruwaym disagreed on the question of preaching Sufism before the uninitiated (*al-ʿāmma*); Junayd asserted that it was worthwhile whereas Ruwaym argued that it was of no avail. Junayd rebuked Shiblī for pronouncing the word *allāh* on a certain occasion, and another time he rebuked him for asking a question.

As for the ecstatic utterances (*shaṭḥiyyāt*) quoted from Abū Yazīd [al-Bisṭāmī] and others, these were uttered under the compulsion of *ḥāl* and the power of intoxication, and so they should be neither accepted nor rejected.

58. Sahl b. ʿAbdallāh said, "There are three kinds of *ʿilm*: *ʿilm* from God which is the science of law, *ʿilm* with God which is the science of Sufi states and *ʿilm* of God which is the knowledge of His attributes and qualities." The science of the inner aspect of religion is derived from the science of the external aspect.

59. [On *ʿilm* as compared with *ʿamal* (praxis), *ʿaql* (in-

tellect), and *maʿrifa* (gnosis).] There is a saying: "He who listens with his ears will relate [what he has learned], he who listens with his heart will preach, and he who practices what he has learned is guided and gives guidance." There is another saying: "*ʿIlm* calls out praxis, but if the latter does not respond, *ʿilm* will go away."

ʿIlm is conception of the object as it is, intellect is capacity and talent for perception by which one can distinguish between true and false, commendable, and repugnant. The learned man (*ʿālim*) should be taken as an example for conduct, and the knower, the man of gnosis, should be a source of guidance. *ʿIlm* is mediated information, whereas gnosis is experience of the senses.

60. [Some sayings in praise of intellect.] The pious would not deceive and the intelligent man cannot be deceived. Intellect keeps man away from destructive things. When passion becomes supreme, intellect disappears. You can distinguish between an intelligent man and a stupid man by the following rule: a stupid man will believe whatever absurdity he is told.

If you need the knowledge of a man, you should not examine his faults.

61. The rules concerning the stage of beginning. The first thing that the *murīd* should do after awakening from the state of carelessness (*ghafla*) is to go to a Sufi shaykh who will guide him to the Sufi way and teach him his rights and obligations.

62. The most appropriate thing for the *murīd* is to choose only pure food, drink, and clothes, for thus he will enhance his inner state. A saying of the Prophet: "To seek the permitted things is an obligation after the [explicit] obligations." One of the Sufis said, "To seek the permitted things is an obligation for people in general and to renounce the permitted things is an obligation of this group [the Sufis] except in case of compelling necessity."

63. The next thing is to fulfil the religious duties which he has neglected, and to correct wrongs which he did to people. (A saying of the Prophet on the above point.) For physical injury [which he caused in the past] he should be punished by retaliation, and for verbal abuses he should ask forgiveness from those whom he wronged. He should then recognize the lower soul (*nafs*) and discipline it by exercises, hardship, fasting, prayers, and vigils.

64. On repentance (*tawba*). He will then be one of the repenters who merit the love of Allah (Quran 2:222 quoted). A saying of the Prophet: "The repenter is the beloved of God." The repenter is one of those whose evil acts God will change into good ones;[31] (there follows a Ḥadīth on this point). Repentance is a religious duty for all Muslims. Failure to repent of a sin is more serious than committing the sin. There is time to repent until death or until the locking of the Gate of Repentance.

65. He should then adhere to moral scrupulosity (*wara'*) in all circumstances and he should know that God takes everything into account.

66. When the *murīd* properly achieves the stations of repentance and scrupulosity and begins the station of renunciation (*zuhd*), then comes the time for him to wear the patched frock (*muraqqa'a*) if he aspires to it. He should observe all necessary observances attached to the wearing of the *muraqqa'a*. Wearing the *muraqqa'a* should not be taken lightly. The wearer of *muraqqa'a* should have disciplined his soul by the rules and have tamed it, and he should have passed the stations. Whoever is not thus qualified should not aspire to the rank of shaykh or *murīd*.

67. On self-examination. The *murīd* should recognize his own faults and know how to remove them. He should control

[31]This idea and the following Ḥadīth are in reference to Quran 25:70.

his soul by exertions and by examination of conscience. He should reveal his inner state to his shaykh and constantly ask for his instruction and advice.

68. The *murīd* should follow the stations (*maqāmāt*) according to their order, and he should not move from one station to another before he has properly accomplished its rules (*ādāb*), for example, he should occupy himself with the station of *zuhd* only when he has completed that of *wara*ʿ. He should follow this course until the actions reach into the heart. One of the Sufis said, "It is nobler to engage in the movements of the heart than to perform outward acts [of worship]." Ḥadīth: the excellence of Abū Bakr's faith came from something which was in his heart, not from much prayer and fasting. When the actions come to take place in the heart, the limbs will be restful.

69. The novice should be heedful of each moment. He should be constantly occupied outwardly with supererogatory devotions and inwardly by aspiration, until inspiration descends upon him.

70. To render service to his brethren is more valuable for the novice than to be engaged in supererogatory prayers. ʿĀ'isha said that the Prophet had always been busy with some charitable work. Abū ʿAmr al-Zujājī said that he had not merited the blessing of Junayd by his constant worship but rather by an act of service, when he cleaned his place.

71. The *murīd* should not leave his shaykh before the eye of his heart opens. The distinctive mark of the *murīd* is "to listen and obey." Distinctive symptoms are suggested so as to recognize falseness on the part of *murīd*, *mutawassiṭ*, and *ʿārif*. Junayd said: "But for the distinctive marks, everyone would have claimed to be pursuing the Sufi way."

72. He should know that *maqām*, *ḥāl*, or any act of worship can be accomplished only by sincerity, namely by keeping

it pure from any ostentation (a saying of the Prophet on this).[32] However, if his acts of worship and *aḥwāl* become publicly known without any ostentatious intention on his part, then this should give no cause for blame. Sincerity can be achieved only by recognizing the worthlessness of mankind.

73. The *murīd* should strive to watch his lower soul (*nafs*) attentively and recognize its qualities because it is the *nafs* that commands evil. The Prophet used to seek refuge in God from the *nafs*. (A saying of ʿAlī b. Abī Ṭālib on the need to watch over the soul constantly.) Abū Bakr al-Warrāq describes the soul as being always ostentatious, in most cases hypocritical, and sometimes idolatrous. A saying of al-Wāsiṭī: "The soul is an idol, looking at it with sympathy is idolatry whereas looking at it with scrutiny is worship." If the soul is excused, it will follow its caprice (Quran 41:51 is quoted.) Two similes on the misleading appearance of the *nafs*: "It is like a glowing coal, it is beautiful in color but it scorches." "It is like clean, quiet water hiding the dirt under it."

74. *Nafs* (the lower soul) is an opposite to God. *Nafs* makes the same demands of obedience and admiration on man as does God. It is a "delicate matter" lodged within this mold [of the body]. The soul is the substratum of blameworthy qualities. The spirit (*rūḥ*) is the mine of good and the soul is the mine of evil. The intellect is the army of the spirit, and success which is granted by Allah is its reinforcement. Capricious desire is the army of the soul, and failure is its reinforcement.[33]

75. All matters are of three kinds: those whose rightness is obvious, so they should be followed; those whose error is

[32]Ostentation is considered here as tantamount to polytheism, because when a man performs an act of worship wishing to demonstrate it, he is not doing it exclusively for the sake of God; rather he is associating others with God.

[33]By contrast with success, which is granted by God, failure is conceived as a state of abandonment, that is, failure to gain God's aid.

obvious, so they should be avoided; those which are dubious, and so should be left aside until the right course becomes clear. If you are in doubt as to which of two things is the best, follow the one which is farthest from your desire. The *murīd* should strive to exchange the blameworthy qualities of his soul for the opposite praiseworthy qualities.

76. The ethics (*ādāb*) of companionship (*ṣuḥba*). It is better to sit alone than with an evil companion, and it is better to sit with a worthy companion than to sit alone. Three sayings of the Prophet on friendship: "Man is in the religion of his friend, therefore you should consider carefully whom you befriend." "A man who mixes with people and endures their evil is superior to one who does not mix with people." "There is no benefit in him who does not befriend others and is not befriended." Abū Ḥafṣ al-Nīsābūrī on the rules of companionship among the Sufis: to respect the shaykhs, to have intimate friendship with their peers, to give advice to younger people, not to associate with people who are not of their kind, to act with altruism (*īthār*), not to accumulate property, and to extend their help to others.

77. The Sufi should associate with people of his kind and those from whom he can benefit. "The man most worthy of your company is he who agrees with your religious beliefs and before whom you are ashamed [for your faults]." He should not associate with people who are opposed to his religious affiliation even if they are related to him. (The story of Noah is cited on this point: God told Noah that his scornful son is not of his family; Quran 11:45–46.)

He should associate with those in whom he has confidence as regards their religion and trustworthiness.

78. The Sufi should undertake to serve his brethren and companions (*khidmat al-ikhwān*)[34] and help them in obtaining

[34]On the emphasis on the value of *khidma* in Sufi ethics, see sections 51 and 70 above.

their sustenance. He should endure their offence and should not rebuke them unless they transgress the law. He should recognize the value of every man. Sufyān b. ʿUyayna said: "Whoever is ignorant of the value of other people is more ignorant of his own value." He also said: "Only he who has no value whatsoever belittles the value of other people." He should correct the faults of his companion and try to guide him to the right way. The Prophet said: "One believer is the mirror of the other." ʿUmar said: "Blessed be the man who would indicate my faults to me."

79. His association with each person should be according to his state and what is appropriate for him: with shaykhs and seniors—with respect and service; with one's peers—with cheerfulness, informality, agreement, kindness, and spontaneity. (Sayings of Abū al-ʿAbbās b. ʿAṭāʾ and Junayd approving of informality among friends. A Ḥadīth praising informality on the part of the Prophet toward Abū Bakr and ʿUmar.)

80. He should not flatter his fellows in what is contrary to the religious requirements. He should acquiesce in the truth; an example cited: ʿUmar accepted the criticism of al-ʿAbbās b. ʿAbd al-Muṭṭalib.

81. Companionship with the young—with compassion, guidance, and instruction. He should warn them when necessary. God reproved the Rabbis for not warning their people (Quran 5:63 quoted).

82. Companionship with the master (*ustādh*) is by obedience, so it is not really companionship but service. Complete obedience and respect toward the master are required. The master in the midst of his followers is like the prophet in the midst of his community. Junayd once answered a question of one of his disciples and the latter expressed objection to the answer; Junayd then said, "If you do not believe in my

words, dissociate yourselves from me."[35] He should behave toward the shaykh like the Companions with the Prophet in following the ethics of the Quran. (Quran 49:1, 49:2, and 24:63 quoted.)

83. Companionship with one's servant. The Sufi should be kind to his servant and should not rebuke him. (A Ḥadīth from Anas b. Mālik about the Prophet's behavior toward him as his servant.)

84. Association with visitors from other places (*ghurabā'*)[36] should be with cheerfulness and good manners and respect, because they honor him by coming to him.

85. Association with ignorant persons should be with patience, good manners, and sympathy. He should recognize the favor of God in not making him like them. Offences by the ignorant should be answered as the prophets did (Quran quoted: 7:61, 7:67, 28:55, 45:14 and 3:186).

Sha'bī was once reviled by someone, and Sha'bī replied, "If what you say of me is true, may God forgive me, and if it is false, may God forgive you."

86. Companionship with one's wife and children should be with compassion. One should instruct them in right conduct. Commentary of Quran 66:6, "Instruct them and teach them and thereby protect them from Hell." In particular, one should behave with his wife according to the rule of God (Quran 2:229 quoted). One should spend upon his family from his lawful earnings.

87. Companionship with young men is reprehensible because of the harms involved in it. Whoever is tried by this experience should safeguard his heart and body from them

[35]This is a quotation from Quran 44:21.

[36]*Gharīb* (sing. of *ghurabā'*) is a person who is away from his home. One of the Sufi ways of self-mortification was *ightirāb*, wandering away from one's home; see section 51 above.

and should prompt them to undertake exercises of self-discipline (*riyāḍāt*) and ethical training, and he should avoid informal behavior with them.[37] The desire of the young to associate with the old is praiseworthy, but the desire of the old for the company of the young is a sign of weakness and stupidity.

88. Companionship with brothers involves agreement in everything, except what is unlawful, and avoiding malice and envy.

89. Association with the ruler (*sulṭān*): one must obey him except in disobedience to God or violation of traditional law (Quran 4:59 quoted). One should pray for the ruler and avoid slandering him. It is meritorious to visit a just ruler; but one should stay away from an unjust ruler except in case of necessity or in order to reprove him. He who has to visit them should pray for them and exhort them and reprove them according to his capacity. Some eminent Sufis used to approach the rulers for the welfare of the people. Ibn ʿAṭā' said: "It is more meritorious to be ostentatious [with regard to one's piety] in order to gain social esteem and thereby be able to assist another Muslim than to act in total sincerity[38] for the sake of one's own salvation."

90. Association with people in general should be according to the example of Abū Ḍamḍam. He used to say: "O Allah, I give my life and my honor to you, I forfeit my honor for your sake; whoever reviles me, I shall not revile him and whoever wrongs me, I shall not wrong him."

91. Every limb has its own special ethics (Quran 17:36 quoted). Good ethics with regard to God is that none of your limbs should move for any purpose save for the pleasure of God.

92. The ethics of the tongue. The tongue should always be

[37]See section 79 above, where informality is recommended among peers.
[38]On the question of sincerity versus ostentation, see section 72 above.

busy in reciting God's names (*dhikr*) and in saying good things of the brethren, praying for them, and giving them counsel. He should not say to them things which they dislike. One should not slander nor talk about things which do not concern him. The tongue was created as an interpreter for the heart. Silence is praiseworthy because it is "a cover for the ignorant and adornment for the intelligent."

93. The ethics of hearing. One should not listen to indecencies and slander. One should listen to things which are religiously beneficial. One should listen attentively to the speaker.

94. The ethics of sight. One should lower one's eyes in order not to see forbidden things; one should also avoid looking at the faults of other people and one's brethren (Quran 40:19 quoted). Immodest glances bring about severe retribution (three sayings). Sight should be used to achieve understanding of God's omnipotence, and it should not be tainted by the desires of the soul. An immodest glance at any person violates the rights of God, because all creatures are His slaves.

95. The ethics of the heart are to observe the exalted states (*aḥwāl*) and to reject base thoughts and to think about God's favors (Quran 3:191 quoted). Ḥadīth: "Meditation for one hour is better than ritual worship for a whole year."

It is of the ethics of the heart to think well of God and of all Muslims and to purify the heart of rancor, deceitfulness, disloyalty, envy, and wrong religious beliefs. The Prophet said: "There is a piece of meat in the body; if it is good, the whole body is good, and if it is corrupt, the whole body is corrupt; that is the heart."

96. The ethics of the hands: to give charity and serve the brethren and not use them in acts of disobedience.

97. The ethics of the legs: not to walk in arrogance and not to use them in acts of disobedience.

98. The first stage of companionship (*ṣuḥba*) is acquaintance, then friendship, then familiarity, then intimacy, then companionship, then brotherhood. *Ṣuḥba* is realized only by inward agreement (Quran 59:14 quoted). *Ṣuḥba* is the loftiest of all modes. The companions of the Prophet were therefore designated by the attribute of companionship rather than by other attributes such as *ʿilm* or *fiqh*, which they also deserved.

99. Of the ethics of the Sufis: there should not occur in their speech "that is mine and that is yours" nor "if this had been so, that would not have happened" nor "perhaps" nor "why did you do this?", for these are the manners of the common people (*ʿawāmm*). There should not be among them borrowing, lending, competition, rivalry, and slandering; rather, each of them should be like son to the older, brother to the equal, father to the younger, and slave to the master.

100. Of their rules of conduct: when they assemble they give priority to one of them (chosen for his excellence in various respects) so that they can rely on his authority. Priority should be given first according to learning and then according to seniority (Ḥadīth). The Prophet accorded priority to the people of Badr (Ḥadīth). Priority is also deserved by those who have met eminent shaykhs.

The most excellent member in the company of Sufis should serve his brethren. *Khidma* (service) is the rank which is next to the rank of shaykh,[39] as the Prophet said: "The chief of a people is their servant."

101. Miscellaneous sayings on companionship. When you associate with a man, you should pay attention to his intellect more than to his theological doctrines, because his religion will benefit him and his intellect will benefit him and you.

You should not befriend a man who is primarily concerned with worldly goods (Quran 53:29 quoted).

[39]Here *khidma* signifies the position of the *khādim* (steward), the person who is in charge of managing the material aspects of a Sufi congregation.

One should not mention other people's faults. When asked about the meaning of *ṣuḥba*, Abū ʿUthmān al-Ḥīrī said that it consisted of acting with generosity, equity, and kindness toward one's friend without expecting reciprocation.

Al-Zaqqāq on *ṣuḥba*: "Befriend him who would know of your secrets like God and yet you can trust him [not to betray your secrets]."

It is harmful to associate with a man before whom one has no shame.

(Three miscellaneous sayings on companionship.)

102. Of their ethics: to avoid haughtiness and aggressive behavior. Abū ʿAlī al-Rūdhabārī said: "To act aggressively against one who is above you is impudence, against one who is your peer, bad manners, and against him who is below you, weakness." Conceit is a sign of the degeneration of one's intelligence.

He who adopts the ethical rules should beware of despising any Muslim. (Two sayings of the Prophet to this effect.) A Sufi saying: "You should willingly accept as a brother whomsoever Allah has accepted in His benevolence as a servant."

103. Rules of conduct in visiting and hospitality. When any of his brethren visit him, the Sufi should give them whatever food or drink he has. A saying of the Prophet: "The host should not despise what he has to present nor should the guest despise whatever is given him." A saying of the Prophet: "It is a noble quality to visit one another for the sake of God (*fī allāh*)." One should give to the guest what is readily available even if it is only a drink of water. (The story of Abraham is quoted as an example of hospitality, Quran 11:69 and 51:27.) When Ḥasan al-Baṣrī had food to serve, he would receive the guest in his home; if not, he would go out to meet him. One should not strive to please a guest in an affected or ceremonious manner. Abū al-Bakhtarī tells about the hospitality of Salmān and quotes the latter, saying, "The Prophet

forbade us to behave in an affected, forced manner (*takalluf*)." Abū Ḥafṣ al-Nīsābūrī visited Junayd in Baghdad and served him with great attention and much ado. Junayd disapproved of this conspicuous behavior; Junayd said, "*Futuwwa* (chivalry) is the renunciation of *takalluf*."

104. Yūsuf b. al-Ḥusayn asked Dhū al-Nūn, "Whom should I befriend?" Dhū al-Nūn answered, "Him who would visit you when you are ill and who would return to you [in forgiveness] when you sin [toward him]."

A saying: "He is not a friend who asks, 'Whither?' when you say to him 'Come along with us!' "

One should avoid foul language, for it stirs up hatred.

A Sufi saying: "Men are of three kinds: one, like food, is indispensable; another, like medicine, you may need occasionally; and still another, like disease, you should try to avoid." One should avoid the company of evil persons. (Four maxims supporting this view.)

105. Their rules of conduct in travels. Abū Ḥafṣ al-Nīsābūrī said that the traveler should observe three rules: he should not prepare food for the trip, he should not plan his way nor try to estimate it and, finally, he should know that God guards him.

106. The most worthy purposes for traveling are listed in order of priority: first, Holy War; then, pilgrimage; then, to visit the Prophet's tomb. Next in rank is to visit the al-Aqṣā mosque. Next comes traveling in search of learning; then, to visit shaykhs and brethren. The Prophet said: "God affirms his love for those who love one another for His sake and who visit one another for His sake;" here follows another saying of the Prophet on the merit of visiting for the sake of God).[40] Then, to repair past wrongs and to ask forgiveness. Then, to learn the stories of the past, that they may serve as an

[40]See section 22 above.

example.[41] Then, traveling may be practiced as a way of self-discipline (to tame the desirous soul) and to achieve anonymity.

107. The Sufi should not travel for amusement, vanity, ostentation, or to seek worldly things. Abū Turāb al-Nakhshabī said that nothing is more injurious to the novices than to travel in the pursuit of their caprice.

He should not travel without the consent and permission of his parents and his master.

If he travels in company, he should walk at the pace of the weakest and stop when a friend stops. He should try as much as possible not to postpone prayer beyond its fixed times.

108. The Sufi should prefer walking to riding except in case of pressing necessity, because his traveling is for self-discipline and for the sake of enhancing his religious state. (A saying of the Prophet on the preference of walking on the pilgrimage rather than riding.) A pious tradition says: "On the way to Mecca the angels embrace those who go on foot, they shake hands with those who have beasts of burden, and they greet from far away those who ride in litters."

If the traveler is in a company, he should serve his companions as much as possible.

109. When the Sufi enters a town, he should visit the Sufi shaykh, if there is one. If not, he should go to the meetingplace of the Sufis. If there are several such places, he should go first to the most important of them. He should prefer to stay in a place that has running water [for ritual washing].

If there is no Sufi brotherhood and no Sufi meetingplace in town, he should stay with one of the people of the town who loves the Sufis and inclines to them most.

110. When he enters a convent, he should turn aside and

[41] The stories of the past referred to here are anecdotes and traditions about Sufi saints. The study of such traditions formed an essential part in the edification of Sufis; see section 165 below.

take off his shoes beginning with the left in taking off and with the right in putting on.[42] Then he should turn to the washing place [to perform the ritual washing] and then perform a prayer of two *rak'as* (bowings). [Only now is he ready to greet those who are present.] If there is a shaykh there, he should turn to him and visit him and kiss his head, but if the guest is a young man, he should kiss the shaykh's hand.

He should sit a while with the shaykh without talking except when the latter asks him a question. If the visitor is equal to the shaykh in religious rank or age, he may talk more freely. After that, the guest should return to his place and the residents [of the convent] should come to visit and greet him. However, in Mecca the guest should visit the residents out of reverence for the sanctuary.

111. The guest should be served whatever food is available without formality (*takalluf*). Nice manners with guests are: to begin with greeting, then to express respect, then to give food, and after that, conversation. (Abraham is presented as a model of proper hospitality; Quran 11:69 is quoted.)

In conversation the Sufi should not ask about worldly affairs but about the shaykhs and the companions and brethren.

112. The traveling Sufi should have with him a leather container or a jug for washing, and the leather container is preferable. One shaykh, when shaking hands with a traveler, used to look for the marks of carrying the container in his hand and fingers, and if he found such marks, he would welcome him and if not, he would disdain him and reject him. One of them said: "When you see a Sufi without container or jug, you should know that he is bound to neglect prayer and to uncover his nakedness whether he wishes it or not." It is recommended

[42]That is, in putting on the slippers or sandals which are to be worn inside the convent; this rule is made more explicit by Najm al-Dīn al-Kubrā; see Meier, "Ein Knigge für Sufi's," pp. 28–29, particularly p. 28, n. 2.

for the traveler to carry with him a stick, a needle, a thread, scissors, a razor, and so on, because the traveler is aided by these things in performing the religious duties properly.[43]

113. When the Sufi wants to travel, it is a matter of proper behavior that he should go around among his brethren and notify them of his departure and take leave of them.

It is recommended that those who are of his community should accompany him to see him off.

On his trip he should strive not to overlook any of the supererogatory recitations and especially not to omit the obligatory prayers.

Abū Yaʿqūb al-Sūsī: "The traveler must have four things, and if not he should not travel. These are: religious learning (*ʿilm*) to direct him, scrupulosity to restrain him, moral character to preserve him, and certitude to carry him."

Ruwaym on the rule of the traveler: "His ambition (*himma*) should not precede his step and wherever he stops, there should he make his station."[44]

114. Their rules in dress. The Prophet spoke in praise of such people who did not care about what they wore. ʿUmar used to shorten the sleeves of his garments. "Whatever the truthful Sufi wears is nice on him, and he will be elegant and dignified in it."

115. It is part of their ethics on this matter of clothes to be satisfied with what they have at any given moment without affectation or preference [of one garment over another]. The

[43]The stick should be used presumably as *sutra*, that is, when setting about to pray outside, the traveler should thrust the stick in the ground in front of him. On this point, see *EI*, s.v. "*sutra*" and *EI*², s.v. "*ʿanaza*."

Scissors and razor are required for cutting the fingernails and for shaving the mustache and the hair of armpits and pudenda. These practices were regarded as commendable customs (*sunna*) of cleanliness.

[44]In the Sufi usage, the term *safar* (traveling) could signify actual traveling or wandering, as well as spiritual progress along the Sufi path of *maqāmāt* (cf. Qushayrī, p. 143, l. 10). Hence, Ruwaym's maxim can also be understood as referring to the inner progress.

Sufis should be content with clothes which will cover their nakedness and protect them from the cold and the heat. Such clothes were not considered as worldly goods by the Prophet.[45] The Sufis do not like to have many clothes, and they give their surplus in charity. The Prophet said: "There are three who will enter paradise without accounting: a man who, when he is washing his garment, has no other one; a man who has no more than one pot on his fireplace; and a man who, when he asks for a drink, is not asked, 'What kind of drink do you want?' " 'Ā'isha said: "The Prophet never prepared two of anything."

116. They should endeavor to keep clean and to be elegant. The Prophet said: "Cleanliness is part of the Faith." The Prophet expressed his displeasure when he saw one of the delegates wearing a dirty garment. He also said: "God detests an unclean person." The Sufis object to the wearing of conspicuous clothes.

117. They seek to derive *baraka* (divine blessing) from the clothes of the shaykhs [by kissing them]. (A Ḥadīth is told about Jarīr b. 'Abdallāh al-Bajalī who kissed a garment of the Prophet.)

118. A certain Sufi preferred to wear two sheets like a consecrated pilgrim (*muḥrim*), but the majority of Sufis disapprove of this habit, except for a *muḥrim* or one who is in Mecca, because it is an ostentatious practice and a display of superiority over one's peers.

They also disapprove of the wearing of a gown except for those of the rank of shaykh, because it is part of the shaykh's distinctive outfit, like the hood, the prayer carpet, and the cap, while the habit of the novice is the mantle.

119. It is recommended to have only one garment. A story is related by Jurayrī about a Sufi who wore the same garment both in summer and winter because he had seen in his dream

[45]See section 207 below.

that Sufis having only one garment were to be especially honored in paradise.

120. (Various Sufi sayings are quoted expressing the idea that the Sufi habit in itself does not reflect the real worth of the person who wears it.)

121. The ethics and manners of eating. (Quran 7:31 is quoted.) One should give the poor to eat from what one is eating. One should say at the beginning of the meal "In the name of God." If one forgets to say "In the name of God" at the beginning, he should say this when he remembers. One should eat from the sides of the bowl and not from the middle "because the *baraka* (mana) descends in its middle."

122. One should not be concerned about the provisions of livelihood nor should one be occupied in seeking, gathering, and storing them. (Quran 29:60 quoted.) The Prophet did not store anything for the morrow. One should not talk much about food because this is gluttony. A saying by Ruwaym on his being unconcerned with what he ate. In eating one should intend to satisfy hunger and give one's soul its due but not its pleasure. The Prophet said: "You owe your soul its due." Food should be taken like medicine [as an unpleasant necessity]. Gluttony should be avoided. One should not find fault in any food nor should one praise it. The Prophet said: "Dissolve your food by reciting God's name (*dhikr allāh*) and by prayer, and do not go to sleep right after the meal lest your heart become hardened." God revealed to David that those hearts which were bound to their desires were screened from Him.

123. The Sufis should not have a set time for eating, they should not make much ado about it and should not prefer plenty of food which is unclean over little which is clean (Quran 18:19 quoted). They should not feed each other nor should anyone of them say to the other "Eat!" except the shaykh, who may say so to those below his rank in order to cheer them up and encourage them to overcome their shyness.

However, the custom of the common people is to bring forth the food and invite those who are present to eat.

124. Sufis eat only food whose source they know. They avoid eating the food of unjust and sinful people. A Ḥadīth: "The Prophet forbade us to accept an invitation to dinner by sinful persons." The Sufis refuse to accept the gifts of women and to eat at their meals.

125. The Sufis do not disapprove of conversation during the meal.[46] More of their rules of conduct in eating: to sit on the left leg, to use the formula "In the name of God," to eat with three fingers, to take small bites and chew well, to lick the fingers and the bowl. One should not look at the morsel taken by a friend. When he finishes his eating, he should say: "Praise be to Allah who has made the provisions of our livelihood more plentiful than our needs." It is not polite to dip one's hand in the food because one can get soiled with it, [one should dip only three fingers].

126. [On eating in company.] A Sufi saying: "Eating with brethren should be with informality (*inbisāṭ*); with foreigners, with nice manners; and with the poor (*fuqarā'*), with altruism." Junayd said: "Eating together is like being nursed together, so you should carefully consider the persons with whom you eat." The Sufis prefer to eat in company. (Three Ḥadīths on the merit of eating in company.) When one eats in company, he should not withdraw from eating as long as the others are eating, especially if he is the head of the group. When the Prophet was eating in company, he would be the last one to finish.

127. One Sufi shaykh was asked what kind of eating was not harmful, and he answered: "For thirty years now I have not eaten anything in compliance with my desire."

[46]Abū al-Najīb is in agreement on this point with both Hujwīrī and Ghazālī, but Najm al-Dīn al-Kubrā has the opposite view; see Meier, "Ein Knigge für Sufi's," p. 32, esp. n. 8.

128. [On the merit of fasting.] The Prophet rebuked a man who burped in his presence, saying: "Those of you who are the most sated in this world will be the most hungry on the day of resurrection." Ḥasan [al-Baṣrī] said: "The temptation of Adam was in eating, and this is also your temptation until the day of resurrection." (Some sayings in praise of hunger are adduced here. A Ḥadīth on the religious merit of being hungry.) It is the advice of the Prophet to consume the strength of the lower soul by hunger and thirst. It is reprehensible to look at food by way of examination. It is also blameworthy to waste time in eating. One Sufi used to have for his breakfast some sips of soup and he used to say, "Time is too precious to be spent on eating."

129. Most Sufis believe that a Sufi should not return any of the food which has been presented to him to the person who serves him; this is especially the rule for a guest, because a guest is not entitled to dispose freely of the food which is given him except by eating it. There are different views of scholars on the question: at what moment precisely does the guest obtain legal possession of the food which is given him. Junayd said: "*Baraka* descends upon the Sufis at their meals because they eat only by way of altruism (*īthār*)."

130. Three obligations of the host and three of the guest. The host should present only licit food, keep the times of prayer, and should not withhold from the guest whatever food he is able to give. The guest should sit where he is told by the host, be pleased with what is given to him, and should not leave without asking permission of the host. The Prophet said: "It is a commendable custom (*sunna*) to accompany the guest to the door of the house."

131. Their ethics in sleep. The Prophet disapproved of prolonged sleep.

One should not sleep in the company of people who are sitting. One should not get used to sleeping in a prostrate position. Whoever tends to snore should get used to sleeping on his side and not on his back.

132. The Sufi should strive to make his sleep for God or in God and not away from God. He who sleeps for God is that person who wants to strengthen himself by his sleep for the performance of the ritual duties (*farā'iḍ*) and the supererogatory prayers (*nawāfil*). The *nawāfil* are particularly efficacious in the latter part of the night (a Ḥadith on this point). He who sleeps in God is the *'ārif* (knower) who is occupied by the remembrance of God and is not overtaken by sleep or slumber, and he would sleep only when sleep comes to him not by his own choice. He who sleeps away from God is the one who is heedless of Him.

133. It is one of their rules to go to sleep in a state of ritual cleanliness and to lie down on the right side. One should then say: "In Your name, O God, I lay down my body and in Your name I raise it up. O God, if You withhold my soul, have mercy on it, and if You release it, guard it as You guard Your upright servants. O God, spare me Your punishment on the day of Resurrection."

One should remember God whenever one wakes up. It is preferable to perform the ritual washing and to pray two *rak'as* before going to sleep. It is objectionable to sleep after the morning prayer and after the *maghrib* (sunset) prayer. He who wishes to have only a little sleep should not drink water except to calm his thirst. If you are with a company of people who go to sleep, you should either do as they do or leave them.

Siesta is recommended to enable one to stay up during the night. "To sleep at the beginning of the day is clumsiness, at the middle of the day, praiseworthy behavior, and at the end of the day, stupidity."

(Two accounts of Sufis who did not lie down for thirty years or more.)

134. Abū Yazīd [al-Bisṭāmī] once stretched out his leg in his cell. A heavenly voice announced to him: "He who sits in the presence of royalty without good manners (*bilā adab*) risks being executed."

135. The rules concerning the Sufi audition (*samāʿ*). (Quran 5:83, 39:18, 30:15 quoted.)[47] The Prophet said: "God did not listen to anything as He listened to *dhikr* recitation by a prophet who has a nice voice." It is told that the Prophet uttered a cry when Quran 73:12 was read before him. In another instance, when Quran 4:41 was recited before him, he wept. A Ḥadīth is told by ʿĀ'isha, that the Prophet, Abū Bakr, and ʿUmar once listened to the singing of her slave girl.

136. Dhū al-Nūn on *samāʿ*: "It [*samāʿ*] is a truthful inspiration which stirs the heart toward the truth, so he who listens to it in a truthful manner will realize the truth, while he who listens to it with [the lust of his] lower soul will become a heretic."[48] Sarī [al-Saqaṭī] mentions three different emotional responses to *samāʿ* on the part of different classes of people. The *samāʿ* stirs or reveals that which is in the heart.

137. *Samāʿ* is beneficial to him whose heart is alive and whose lower soul is dead. One of the Sufis said that he had seen al-Khiḍr in his dream and al-Khiḍr said: "*Samāʿ* is a slippery stone on which only the feet of the learned men can stand firmly."

138. It is one of their rules not to behave in an affected manner in the *samāʿ* and not to have a fixed time for it. They should not listen for the purpose of enjoying or diverting

[47]These verses are obviously quoted here to prove that it is lawful to give vent to one's emotions upon hearing a recitation of the Quran. The two traditions about the Prophet in this section are also adduced for this purpose.

[48]Translation hardly gives the full range of meaning suggested by the Arabic. The key word in this saying is *ḥaqq*, (truth) which is repeated four times; *ḥaqq* also means "what is rightfully yours," and in this sense it is the opposite of *ḥaẓẓ* (desire or sensual pleasure) which is connected with the lower soul. Used with the definite article, *al-ḥaqq* is one of the names of God, the Real One.

themselves. They should listen to such things that will prompt them to pious actions and will rejuvenate their aspiration.

The Sufis must learn the rules pertaining to *samāʿ*. Abū ʿAmr b. Nujayd said: "To make one mistake in *samāʿ* is worse than to slander people for years."

139. It is improper to induce deliberately the state of ecstasy or to constrain oneself to rise up [to dance],[49] except if one is overcome by ecstasy or in order to help by way of solidarity a fellow who is in a state of ecstasy.

One may also do this by way of cheering himself without pretending to be intoxicated or affecting ecstasy, but it is better to avoid this. (A Ḥadīth is adduced against showing the emotions which are stirred by listening.)

140. It is disapproved for young men to rise up at the presence of shaykhs and show their ecstasy. A young disciple of Junayd used to get into ecstasy whenever he listened to *samāʿ*. Junayd forbade him to give vent to his ecstatic emotions and the young man controlled himself, but one day he died in a moment of rapture. There is no dispensation (*rukhṣa*) whatever permitting adolescents to rise up and move [to dance][50] in *samāʿ* sessions, and most shaykhs disapprove altogether of their being present at *samāʿ* sessions.

141. When a moment of real ecstasy occurs, the person who participates by his own effort[51] should not enter the dance, not even by way of solidarity. (A narrative about Dhū al-Nūn and a Sufi who affected ecstasy.)

To remain quiet, yet keep the heart attentive, is better than constrained participation in the dance because this is the oc-

[49]In theory, dancing was acceptable only as a result of ecstasy but not as an inducement to it; see on this matter Meier, "Der Derwischtanz, Versuch eines Überblickes," *Asiatische Studien* 8 (1954), 127.

[50]See section 174 below.

[51]That is, a person who is not spontaneously stirred by the *samāʿ*.

casion of "stability." To listen attentively is one of the rules of behavior when in the divine presence (Quran 46:29 and 20:108 quoted).

142. The *samāʿ* session should begin and close with recitations from the Quran.

143. It is disapproved for the *murīd* to listen to love poems and erotic descriptions. Only the knower (*ʿārif*) can properly practice *samāʿ*. A saying by Junayd: "If a novice is attracted to *samāʿ*, you can know that there is still in him a remainder of falseness." The *samāʿ* is [like the] *ṣirāṭ* bridge; it may lead some to the loftiest heights and throw others to the lowest depths. The *samāʿ* is more suitable for shaykhs than for novices.

144. A person who smiles or amuses himself should not be present at a *samāʿ* session. (A narrative by ʿAbdallāh b. Khafīf about his master Aḥmad b. Yaḥyā as an example.)

145. Each mental faculty enjoys something in the *samāʿ*: the heart, words of wisdom; the spirit, melody; the lower soul, the mention of sensual pleasures which suit its nature.

146. Affected behavior in *samāʿ* may be of two different kinds. A person may act in an affected way to gain social respect or some other worldly benefit, and in this case it is deceit. On the other hand, a man may act in this way in quest of "the reality" (*al-ḥaqīqa*), seeking ecstasy (*wajd*) by means of artificial ecstasy (*tawājud*). The relationship between *wajd* and *tawājud* is the same as between "weeping" and "trying to weep"; the Prophet said: "When you see people suffering, you should weep, and if you do not weep, then try to weep."

147. [Miscellanea on *samāʿ*.] People who participate in *samāʿ* are of three classes. First there are those who refer, when they are listening, to what is communicated to them from the Real One (*al-ḥaqq*). Then there are those who refer, when they are listening, to what is communicated to them by means of their states, stations, and moments of experience. The third

class are the poor (*fuqarā'*)[52] who have entirely detached themselves from worldly things; *samā'* is suitable for them.

It is said that only one whose state is weak needs the *samā'* [to arouse his spirit], but the vigorous one does not need it. One of the Sufis said: "How low is the state of a person who needs someone to stir him! Upon my life, a bereaved mother does not need a mourner."

Samā' has a different effect on different types of people. *Samā'* is like weapons which can serve good or bad purposes, or it is like the sun which has a good effect on some things and a bad effect on others.

Samā' is [an experience] on the part of the listener.[53] A Sufi once heard a peddler announcing, "*Yā sa'tar barrī!*" (Oh, wild thyme), and he fainted. When he was later asked about this, he answered, "I thought that he was announcing "*Is'a tara birrī*" (exert yourself and you will see My benevolence).

Ṣubayḥī said: "A person who is in a state of true ecstasy should not be rebuked for what he may utter in his ecstatic state."

Ecstasy is the secret of the inner qualities, just as obedience is the secret of the external qualities.

148. Concerning the Sufi mantles (*khiraq*, pl. of *khirqa*) which are thrown off during the *samā'*.[54] If they are thrown off

[52]Here *fuqarā'* clearly signifies regular Sufis of the lower ranks of initiation; cf. Introduction above.

[53]I.e., the influence of *samā'* depends on the spiritual state of the hearer, hence it is a subjective experience. This idea is more explicitly stated by Sarrāj, see Sarrāj, "Abstract of Contents," p. 76. The Sufis tended to be impressed by things which they heard accidentally and which they took as referring to them personally; this is clearly exemplified in the Sufi anecdote mentioned here. On this question, see Meier, "Der Derwischtanz," p. 118.

[54]Sections 148-151 are concerned with the custom of taking off the Sufi mantle (*khirqa*) and throwing it into the middle of the circle during the *samā'*. The custom itself is well known (see Meier, "Der Derwischtanz," p. 125); Abū al-Najīb assumes that this practice is recognized and acceptable, and he dis-

[in a communal session] by way of solidarity [with other Sufis who are in a state of real ecstasy], they belong to the Sufi group. If the mantle is thrown off in a state of ecstasy induced by the recitation of a reciter, not in a communal session, it should belong to the reciter. However, if it takes place [under the effect of recitation] in a communal session, there are two opinions on how to divide the thrown mantles. According to one opinion, they belong to the reciter; according to another, they belong to the whole group, with the reciter taking his share along with the rest of the group. The division of the *khiraq* is held comparable to the division of booty (a Ḥadīth is quoted on the equal division of the booty by the Prophet after the battle of Badr). Some say that if the reciter is himself a Sufi, he should take a share in the division as one of them. However, if he is not one of them, he should receive from it whatever is of value; but the rags of the Sufis belong to the Sufis.[55] Some make a further distinction [in case the reciter is not one of the Sufi community]: if he is hired, he should not receive any part of it; but if he is a volunteer, he should get whichever of the clothes that may be useful to him.

149. When the *khiraq* which have been thrown belong to the participants, they should not occupy themselves with the division until the *samāʿ* is over. If an admirer of the Sufis is present, he may redeem the *khiraq* by any amount that he spontaneously feels called upon to give.[56] But the *khiraq* should not be offered for sale nor auctioned off, because to do so would

---

cusses in detail the question of how to divide the clothes that were thrown off and torn.

[55]The Sufi mantles, which are taken off in the state of ecstasy, are believed to be impregnated with *baraka*.

[56]Jīlānī set himself most strongly against this custom (of which Suhrawardī approved), namely, that a rich admirer "redeem" the Sufi clothes for cash and then give them back to the Sufis. Jīlānī considered this practice a tricky way of begging (see *Al-Ghunya li-Ṭālibī Ṭarīq al-Ḥaqq*, 2 vols. in one (Cairo: Muṣṭafā al-Bābī al-Ḥalabī, 1375/1956), II, 181, ll. 19ff.).

be to hold cheap the value of the *khiraq* and to underrate the worth of the Sufis themselves.

150. If a shaykh is present, he should give judgment on what to do with the clothes: to tear, exchange, or return to the owner. The Syrians say that each Sufi has a right to receive back his *khirqa*, but most of the Sufis disapprove of this opinion. Some say that it is better to return those garments that were thrown off by way of solidarity or affectation.[57] Most shaykhs dislike the throwing of the *khirqa* by way of solidarity, because this is constrained behavior, which is removed from the truth.

151. If no shaykh is present there, they themselves should rule on this matter spontaneously. They approve of tearing the "patched mantles" (*muraqqaʿāt*) only for the purpose of deriving *baraka* from them. It is preferable to tear to pieces the *khiraq* of the regular Sufis, if they can be used for patching, so that each one can get his share. These pieces should be distributed to those who are present in the *samāʿ*, to the exclusion of the absentees,[58] because booty is divided among those who are present in the battle. If others [who are not regular Sufis] are present, then those who are lay members (*muḥibbūn*) should be given a share of the torn pieces.

The opinions of the shaykhs vary on how to divide. Some hold that they should be divided according to some principle of preference, like inheritances and booty. Others maintain that if the division is made by a shaykh, he may divide in unequal parts, but if they divide among themselves, they should divide equally.

That which is not suitable for making patches should better be given without tearing it to a deserving poor man. As for the clothes of the lay members [which were thrown off in the *samāʿ*], it is better to sell them or give them to the reciter rather than to tear them to pieces.

[57]The reason being clearly that such garments are not impregnated by the *baraka* (mana) which results from ecstasy.

[58]I.e., those members of the Sufi congregation who did not attend that session.

152. Their ethics in marriage. One should prefer a woman who is pious and upright. The Prophet said: "A woman may be married for her piety, property, and beauty; choose a pious woman and you will be rich." Another saying of the Prophet: "The best wife is she who requires the least provision." ʿUmar b. al-Khaṭṭāb said: "Women are made of feeble minds and lustful desires; you should treat their feeble minds by silence and their desires by confining them to the house."

Their rule in this matter [of marriage] is not to marry for this-world's reasons nor to marry a rich woman; rather, one's purpose in marriage should be to comply with the established custom (*sunna*) and to preserve one's chastity.

153. The husband should satisfy his wife's needs according to his capability, but if he is unable to provide for her needs, or if she demands more than is in his power, he should let her choose between accepting what he can give her and divorce, following the example of the Prophet. (A Ḥadīth is cited about the choice proposed by the Prophet to his wives, quoting Quran 33:28 and 33:52.)

154. In our times it is better to avoid marriage[59] and to suppress desire by discipline, hunger, vigils, and traveling. A pious man was once asked why he did not get married, and he answered, "I have a lower soul which I would repudiate if I could, so should I add to it another one?" (Four sayings against marriage, particularly on account of the hardship of providing for the family.) A wise man should not disclose the secret faults of his wife nor of a woman he has divorced.

The marriage of ʿAlī b. Abī Ṭālib and Fāṭima is cited as an example of virtuous marriage. ʿAlī said: "We possessed

[59]Abū al-Najīb's opinion on this issue seems to be in agreement with the opinion of Ghazālī, who says that the *murīd* should not get married; see Ghazālī, *Iḥyāʾ ʿUlūm al-Dīn*, 4 vols. (Cairo: Muṣṭafā al-Bābī al-Ḥalabī, 1358/1939), III, 98, l. 3, and 100, l. 12. By contrast, Jīlānī considers marriage to be an absolute obligation (*Ghunya*, I, 43).

nothing but the skin of a ram on which we used to sleep at night, and at daytime we would feed the water-carrying camel on it."

155. A chapter on the ethics of begging. (Quran 2:273 and 93:10 are quoted.) It is obligatory to give to a beggar. On the other hand, if a person does not need to beg or is strong and healthy he should not beg. ʿUmar said: "A source of earning which is somewhat dubious is better than begging." Junayd said: "Any Sufi who has accustomed himself to seek means of livelihood in times of hardship has not freed himself from the servitude of his lower soul and is not sustained by forbearance." Abū Ḥafṣ [al-Nīsābūrī] said: "Whoever is in the habit of begging is afflicted with greed, disloyalty and lying."

156. Their rules in this matter of begging are: to beg only in time of pressing need and to take only as much as necessary. A Sufi saying: "When a Sufi is constrained to beg, his atonement is his veracity." One should not reject a beggar.

157. The Sufis detest begging for themselves but consider it meritorious to beg for one's companions. They do not consider this [begging for others] to be begging, because this is the seeking of aid for charity and piety. The Prophet used to beg for his companions. It is meritorious to forfeit one's social honor for the sake of one's brethren. The rule for whoever is charged with collecting charity is that he should not think of himself in either taking or giving but rather should act as an agent for both parties. An anecdote is told by way of an example: When people from other places would come to visit the shaykh Abū al-ʿAbbās al-Nihāwandī, he would go to the market and gather whatever food was available and would bring it to them. And he used to say, "For twenty years I have not taken anything from anyone." He used to detest begging and disapproved of it.

Junayd said: "Begging should not be practiced except by a person who likes better to give rather than to take." It is better for the Steward (*khādim*)[60] to borrow what he needs to spend on his community, and afterwards he can beg to pay his debt.

158. Some Sufis allow begging as a dispensation for whoever intends to humiliate himself in this manner. One shaykh used to eat only what he received by begging; when asked about it, he said: "I chose this because my soul (*nafs*) detests it." The Sufi should beg only in time of need; when he begs, his words are directed at the people but his heart should be directed toward the Real One. A saying: "Free men strive for the sake of their brethren, not for themselves." A saying: "It is better to eat by begging than by asking hospitality." Whoever begs even though he has enough will be asked to account for it on the Day of Resurrection.

159. Their conduct in illness. The Prophet said: "A fever for one day is atonement for a year." One of the sages said: "In illness there are benefits which the intelligent man should not ignore: a purging of sin, an opportunity to deserve the reward for forbearance, an awakening from heedlessness, a reminder of God's favor in the state of health, a renewal of repentance, and an inducement to give charity." One shaykh said: "I would rather be healthy and thank Allah than be afflicted and endure." The Prophet said that one should seek medication in case of illness because medication, like illness, is of God's judgment.

160. Their rules of behavior on the deathbed. The Prophet said: "Remember the destroyer of pleasure." At his death the Prophet cried: "O, my grief!" (The meaning of this cry is explained in various ways because it could not possibly result from lack of endurance on the part of the Prophet.) Jurayrī describes the conduct of Junayd in his deathbed: he persisted in reading the Quran to his last moment.

An anecdote on Khayr al-Nassāj. While he was dying he

[60]On the meaning of *khādim*, see section 100, n. 39 above.

said, "You [Death] are a slave charged with orders and I am a slave charged with orders; what you were ordered to do, you will not miss, but what I was ordered to do, I may miss." So he called for water, performed the ritual ablution, and prayed; then he pronounced the formula *allāhu akbar* (God is the most great) and died.

ʿAlī b. Sahl used to say: "Do you believe that I will die like those sick people? Rather, I will be called and I shall respond." As he was sitting one day he suddenly said, "*Labbayka*," and he died.[61]

161. An anecdote about the death of Aḥmad b. Khaḍrawayh: He did not want to die before paying his debts, and at the last moment a miraculous messenger paid them.

(A series of anecdotes about famous Sufis in their last hours.)

162. An anecdote on Shiblī: he was concerned with meticulous observance of the *sunna* even as he was dying. An account by Ibn ʿAbbās about ʿAmr b. al-ʿĀṣ on his deathbed and his last conversation with his pious son ʿAbdallāh. ʿAmr described to his son the agony of dying; his last words were: "O, Allah, You commanded and I disobeyed. You prohibited and I committed. I am not innocent so that I might excuse myself nor am I powerful so that I might vindicate myself, but 'There is no god except Allah!' " (The last words of the Caliph ʿAbd al-Malik b. Marwān are quoted.)

163. Their ethics in times of affliction (*balā*ʾ). (Quran 20:40 is quoted. Four sayings of the Prophet on the worth of *balā*ʾ.) Their ethics in this matter are not to show grief nor to complain but rather to see the benefit of being afflicted, which is the prospect of reward for him who endures the trial with forbearance (Quran 39:10).

164. One must consider that the affliction is brought upon him by God and then one will not suffer the pain of it. (Quran

[61] *Labbayka,* meaning "at your service," is the phrase pronounced by the pilgrims upon entering the holy area of Mecca.

52:48 is quoted.) The women in the story of Joseph did not feel the pain of cutting their hands because they were occupied in watching him (Quran 12:31 quoted). When one looks at his beloved, it is easier to endure the pain. (Verses of Majnūn Banī ʿĀmir [Majnūn Laylā] and by Abū al-Shīṣ about their sufferings for the sake of their love.) The true Sufi should also suffer patiently like them. A saying of Ḥusayn b. ʿAlī (in reference to another saying by Abū Dharr al-Ghifārī): "He who relies on the choice of God does not wish anything for himself except whatever God may choose for him." (An anecdote about Shiblī when he was confined to an asylum.)

165. The Sufis should endure affliction with strength and patience. A Ḥadīth: God prefers a strong Muslim to a weak one. So you should try to preserve what is beneficial to you with God's help, but if some evil befalls you, you should say: "This is God's predestination and whatever He wills He does." Do not say: "If it were" (*law*), because *law* starts the action of Satan.[62]

Ibn ʿAṭāʾ said: "It is in times of trial that you can distinguish between false claims and true claims." (Quran 29:1–3 and 47:31 are quoted.) Affliction for man is like tanning [to a hide], it removes all his frivolities and brings him to a state of usefulness. Junayd on affliction: "It is a lamp for the knowers, an awakening for the novices, and a destruction for the heedless." Jaʿfar al-Ṣādiq used to say when affliction came upon him: "O, Allah, I pray that this be by way of moral instruction and not on account of wrath." There can be different purposes for *balāʾ*: it may come as a purge of sins, as a means of moral education, as a trial, or as a punishment and a sign of abandonment.[63]

The stories of the Sufis are valuable because only through

[62]*Law* (the particle introducing a rejected condition) implies dissatisfaction with God's decree. See section 99 above.

[63]On the concept of "abandonment," see section 74, n. 33 above.

them can one learn their way of conduct in times of distress. Junayd upholds the value of Sufi stories for the edification of novices, quoting Quran 11:120 in support of his opinion.[64]

PART IV

166. A chapter on the rules on *rukhaṣ* (dispensations).[65] The Prophet said: "God wishes that His dispensations be practiced just as He wishes that His strict rules (*ʿazāʾim*) be observed." In answer to a question by ʿUmar b. al-Khaṭṭāb on a certain dispensation, the Prophet said: "It is charity which God granted you, and you should accept His charity."

The *rukhaṣ* should be only a temporary repose. The *rukhaṣ* form a border area between the licit and the prohibited; whoever falls short of the level of *rukhaṣ* falls into error and ignorance.

According to the doctrine of the Sufis, the practice of the *rukhaṣ* signifies a withdrawal from the reality of religion to the externality of religion, and that is a decline in religious state.[66] Dhū al-Nūn said: "The ostentation of the knowers is the sincerity of the novices."[67] An anecdote about Junayd which teaches the following lesson: the more saintly the man, the more strictly he will be judged. One of "the people of the portico" (*ahl al-ṣuffa*)[68] died and left two dirhams; when this was told to the Prophet, he said: "These are two burns on

[64]See section 106 above.

[65]On the significance of *rukhaṣ*, see Introduction above.

[66]See Introduction above. It must be noted that in order to understand the social or ethical significance of each "dispensation" the dispensation should be considered as an exception or contradiction—ostensibly at least—of a more general rule or principle. In the apparatus of my edition of the Arabic text reference to such contrasting parallels is made.

[67]The point of this saying is that there are different standards of religious accomplishment; what would not be acceptable on the part of a knower can be permitted a novice.

[68]See section 40, n. 24 above.

him!"[69] When the Prophet said: "Whoever assumes resemblance to a group of people is one of them," he intended assumption of their way of life, not of their dress. He also said: "Whoever imitates a group of people in his manner of speech and dress while his acts are incompatible with his appearance, that person is accursed by Allah and the angels and by all men."

The Sufis have rules and ethics concerning the *rukhaṣ*, and he who wishes to practice the *rukhaṣ* must know these rules and hold fast to them. This is necessary in order that he may follow the customs of the Sufis and be embellished by their embellishment, until he may reach the stations and the states of those Sufis who attain to the reality.

167. It is allowed by way of *rukhṣa*[70] to possess an estate or to rely on a regular income.[71] Their rule in this matter is that one should not use all of it for himself, but should dedicate this to public charities and should take from it only enough for one year for himself and his family, following the example of the Prophet.

168. There is a *rukhṣa* allowing one to be occupied in business; this dispensation is granted to him who has to support a family. But this should not keep him away from the regular performance of prayers. He should not consider this activity as a means of earning his livelihood but as a way of helping other Muslims. He should try to limit his business hours to the period between the morning prayer and the noon

[69]For, as one of "the people of the portico," this man had a claim to be considered a complete ascetic; this claim was disproved by the two dirhams which he left, and hence he could be blamed for falsehood.

[70]In the Arabic this section begins with the phrase *fa-min rukhaṣihim* (it is one of their dispensations); the following 39 sections (168-206) all begin with *wa-minhā* (and one of them is).

[71]This is contrary to the rule given by Qushayrī: "The novice should not have any regular income, no matter how small." (Qushayrī, p. 203, l. 23). However, the present dispensation is apparently intended not for the regular novice but for the "lay member"; cf. Introduction, n. 61 above.

prayer, so that he can pray all five daily prayers with his companions.

If he gains more than he needs for his family, he should give it to the members of his brotherhood (*ahl ṣuḥbatihi*).[72]

169. There is a *rukhṣa* allowing one to beg. The rules of this *rukhṣa* are: One should not beg except in time of need and only as much as is necessary to provide for those who depend on him.

One should not humiliate himself in begging (some verses by Jaʿfar al-Ṣādiq are quoted against humiliating oneself before other men).

One should not make begging a habit or a regular source of income.

170. There is a *rukhṣa* according to which one may borrow money while referring to God as guarantor. However, this should be done for charitable purposes or for the brethren or under compelling necessity (*ḍarūra*). One should not fail to be concerned about returning the debt.

171. There is a *rukhṣa* allowing one to carry food provisions on travel. The rule is that one should be generous with them to others in his company.

172. There is a *rukhṣa* according to which one may perform a pilgrimage on behalf of another person for payment; however, it is permissible to receive wages for this only in time of pressing necessity. One should use this payment for his expenses on his way without resorting to begging or to the use of pious endowments.

173. There is a *rukhṣa* allowing one to travel about the land.[73] The rule is that the purpose of such traveling should be to visit one of the brethren or to ask forgiveness or to seek religious learning.

[72]It should be noted that the word *ṣuḥba* (companionship) is used also to signify "a Sufi community" or "brotherhood"; for the same usage, see section 113 above.

[73]See section 107 above.

174. There is a *rukhṣa* according to which one may rise up and move in the *samāʿ*.[74] The rule in this matter is to behave in accordance with the spirit of the moment. One should avoid affected participation [in the dance] when this is [for the other dancers] a time of earnest ecstasy. However, when this [dancing] is for cheering up, it is permissible [to dance] in order to help others, without pretending to be intoxicated or affecting ecstasy.[75]

175. There is a *rukhṣa* allowing one to joke. The rule in this matter is to avoid slandering, imitation, and nonsense. ʿAlī said: "When the Prophet saw one of his friends distressed, he would cheer him up by joking."

It is improper, especially for persons of high rank, to do much jesting. It is said: "Do not jest with a noble man lest he bear malice against you, and do not jest with a base person lest he behave impudently toward you."

176. There is a *rukhṣa* allowing one to speak publicly about aspects of the religious sciences which one has not yet practiced. The condition for this dispensation is that the purpose of such speaking should be to give counsel and guidance.[76]

177. There is a *rukhṣa* according to which Sufis may wear patched frocks (*muraqqaʿāt*) which are artificially made; however, they should avoid conspicuousness and should not waste time on this. Whenever the Sufi masters saw a Sufi who

[74]This is an allusion to the Sufi dance. Some Sufis objected to applying the word *raqṣ* (dancing) to the Sufi dance, because the word *raqṣ* was associated with a secular, quite reprehensible, type of experience, Cf. Hujwīrī, *Kashf al-Maḥjūb*, p. 416.

[75]See sections 139 and 141 above.

[76]It was a generally recognized principle that religious knowledge which is not matched with practice is worthless. Accepting this principle, the Sufis had to face the question of whether a Sufi should be allowed to speak about those aspects of the Sufi doctrine which he had not yet experienced. It appears that there was no unanimity on this matter (see section 55 above), but the general principle was that a *novice* should not speak about that which he had not experienced.

indulged excessively in embellishing his patched frock and other clothes, they disdained him. It is recommended to follow the middle way in this matter.

178. There is a *rukhṣa* according to which friends may embrace and kiss each other upon meeting. The rule is that it should be only among peers and people who are on intimate terms. The Prophet said: "Embracing is a way of confirming love."

179. There is a *rukhṣa* allowing one to love leadership. The ethics of this matter are that one should know one's own capability and should not have aspirations beyond it. Anonymity is better for the ignorant than fame. One should not seek what he cannot obtain lest he lose what he has. One of the shaykhs said: "The fault which is the last to leave the heart of the righteous is the love of leadership."

180. There is a *rukhṣa* allowing one to associate with Sultans and to visit them. The rule in this is that the Sufi should not be deluded by the praise lavished on him, and if he is praised contrary to what he knows of himself, he should shun that praise. God rebukes those who like to be praised for what they have not done (Quran 3:188 is quoted). From this, it can be inferred that if a person likes to be praised for what he *has* done, this is not a sin. However, this is a harmful thing, of which one should beware. In such an instance [that is, when being praised] one should say: "O, God, render me better than what they consider me; forgive me what they do not know of me and do not blame them for what they say."

181. There is a *rukhṣa* allowing one to revile insolent persons by disparaging their ancestors. The rule is that one may resort to this *rukhṣa* only in retort to ill-behavior, and it should be done by indirect expressions and not by explicit ones.

182. There is a *rukhṣa* according to which one may exhibit good works and acts of worship. The rule is that it should be

for the purpose of setting an example. But one should not pay attention to agreement or objection on the part of people. When asked about this matter, the Prophet said [quoting Quran 2:271]: "If you publish your acts of charity, it is good." This verse refers to supererogatory rituals and good works,[77] but as for the obligatory rituals, there is unanimous agreement that it is better to display them publicly.

183. There is a *rukhṣa* according to which one may go out [of society] in order to remove oneself from its evils. If one chooses to withdraw from society, one should repair to a solitary place in a cave or a wadi or some other place which is free from anything evil.[78]

184. There is a *rukhṣa* allowing one to watch all kinds of amusement. This is, however, limited by the rule: What you are forbidden from doing, you are also forbidden from watching.

185. There is a *rukhṣa* according to which one may attend sessions in which people are engaged in worthless talk. However, one should avoid listening to calumny and objectionable things.

186. There is a *rukhṣa* allowing one to eat tasty food. The rule of this dispensation is: It should be only between periods of hunger and exertion. (Four Ḥadīths are quoted in proof that the Prophet did not abstain from good food.)[79]

187. There is a *rukhṣa* allowing one to pledge one's clothes for food; however, only in time of necessity.

188. There is a *rukhṣa* allowing one to escape abasement

[77]The rest of this verse, referred to here but not quoted in full by Abū al-Najīb, is "but if you conceal them . . . that is better for you."

[78]It is noteworthy that retirement from society is presented by Abū al-Najīb as a "dispensation"; he thereby indicates that the normal way of life for the Sufi is that of association with other people.

[79]Two of these traditions praise the eating of meat; they are apparently adduced in order to take exception to Sufis who abstained from meat, cf. Ibn al-Jawzī, *Talbīs Iblīs* (Cairo: Maṭbaʿat al-Saʿāda, 1340 A.H.), p. 223, and p. 226, l. 16.

and the suffering of offense. This should be done in order to keep one's mind free from evil thoughts and to avoid enmity. One of the Sufi masters said: "Escaping from that which cannot be tolerated is a commendable custom of the prophets" (he then quoted Quran 26:21 as an example). The Prophet said: "The Muslim should not debase himself."

189. There is a *rukhṣa* allowing one to visit friends without having been invited. [Such visits are characteristic of the informality which is held to be the standard of behavior among peers.] They should choose for such informal visits those who are delighted by this informality and recognize the honor of it.

190. There is a *rukhṣa* according to which one may reprimand one's brethren. However, this should be done for the purpose of eliminating malice from the heart and not by way of revenge. Further, one should accept the apology of a friend. It is better to reprimand frankly than to bear rancor secretly.

191. There is a *rukhṣa* according to which one may praise what he previously blamed and blame what he previously praised.

192. There is a *rukhṣa* allowing one to dissociate himself from those who rightly should be excommunicated. The rule of this dispensation is that the purpose of such treatment should be to reveal the truth and eradicate falsehood and to show enmity for the sake of God. The Prophet excommunicated Kaʿb b. Mālik and his two friends for staying away from the raid on Tabūk (Quran 9:118 is quoted).

193. There is a *rukhṣa* according to which one may tear the patched frock (*muraqqaʿa*) of fake Sufis. The purpose of such action should be to eradicate their misrepresentation and deceit (Quran 16:94 is quoted). The *muraqqaʿa* worn by a fake Sufi is comparable to the false [long] hair worn by one who fraudulently represents himself as belonging to the house

of ʿAlī;[80] in both these cases one should expose the falsehood of such imposters.

The Prophet ordered the destruction of the mosque of the dissenters, because he knew that although it was, in appearance, a mosque, it was, in fact, intended for spreading dissension and disbelief (Quran 9:108 is quoted). He also ordered the palm trees of Banū Naḍīr cut down. Although such destruction is, as a rule, prohibited, yet this particular act was allowed by Allah (Quran 59:5 is quoted).

194. There is a *rukhṣa* allowing one to lie in the interest of worthy causes. The story of Abraham (Quran 21:63) and the story of David (Quran 38:23) are referred to as examples. An anecdote about a dispute between Jaʿfar al-Ṣādiq and a Murji'ite: Jaʿfar al-Ṣādiq used a lie as a rhetorical device in order to prove the absurdity and the error of the Murji'ite position.

195. There is a *rukhṣa* to visit old women. The purpose of such a visit should be to seek God's favor and blessing and to pray.

196. There is a *rukhṣa* according to which one may behave with affected politeness with rich and powerful persons. However, the purpose of this should not be to gain any material benefit or honor from them.

197. There is a *rukhṣa* allowing one to cry when one is hit by calamity. However, this should be done without mournful wailing, nor should it be in a loud voice. The Prophet cried when his son Ibrāhīm died.

198. There is a *rukhṣa* allowing one to keep company with young men. The rule of this dispensation has been mentioned above in the chapter on companionship (*ṣuḥba*).[81]

199. There is a *rukhṣa* according to which one may show

[80]Those who claimed to be of ʿAlid descent wore their hair conspicuously long. See Ghazālī, *Iḥyā'*, I, 139–140.

[81]See section 87 above.

a smiling face to a person whom he dislikes in his heart. The purpose of such an affected manner should be the quest of peace rather than ostentation or hypocrisy.

ʿĀ'isha tells the following Ḥadīth: "A certain man asked permission to enter to see the Prophet while I was with the Prophet, and the Prophet said, 'What an evil man!' and then he admitted him and spoke to him in a placatory manner. I marveled at this behavior, and when the man had left I asked the Prophet about it and he answered: 'O ʿĀ'isha, the worst of persons is one whom you treat with respect for fear of his foul tongue.' "

200. There is a *rukhṣa* allowing one to behave with riffraff in a manner which is compatible with their worth and intellectual capacity, in order to keep safe from their dangers.

201. There is a *rukhṣa* according to which one may obtain the assistance of rude, insolent persons in times of disaster and in order to ward off harm. The rule in this matter is that the purpose of such association should be to protect oneself and one's dignity from confronting persons who are not of his kind. It is said that Ibn ʿUmar liked to have an impudent person in his company so that this impudent man would defend him from the insolence of others.

202. There is a *rukhṣa* allowing one to mention the faults of people. However, one should only mention those defects which are publicly well known.

203. There is a *rukhṣa* according to which one may placate poets and others like them by paying them. Such a course of action may be taken in order to protect one's reputation and safeguard one's religion from them, so that they do not slander him. The Prophet said: "Whatever a man spends to protect his reputation is considered charity."

204. There is a *rukhṣa* according to which one may plunder the food which is scattered at banquets.[82] One should, however

[82] Jīlānī, too, mentions the custom of scattering food at wedding banquets

do so without gluttony and with the intention of delighting the host. A Ḥadīth quotes the Prophet saying: "I only forbade you to plunder armies but I did not forbid you to plunder banquets."

205. There is a *rukhṣa* according to which one is allowed to boast and to publish his claims [of merit]. If one acts in this manner it should be with the intention of revealing the favors which God has bestowed on him; as He said [Quran 93:11]: "And as for the grace of your Lord, declare it."

This manner of boasting is allowed only under the effect of ecstasy or in a contest of boasting with some rival.

(Ḥadīths are quoted to show that the Prophet spoke in a boastful manner when he was in a state of ecstasy and when he was engaged in a contest against adversaries.)

206. There is a *rukhṣa* allowing one to show annoyance and exasperation upon encountering that which is absurd and which should not be tolerated. Such annoying things can be either words or actions. However, one should avoid the use of foul language and attempt to protect his own right without transgressing its limits to do injustice [to others], because when anger gains control, it overcomes reason.

One should try not to get angry for one's own rights; rather, if one gets angry, it should be out of jealousy for the rights of God and of one's brethren. It is said that the Prophet never sought to take revenge for a wrong done to him, but only took revenge on those who had violated the prohibitions of God.

207. [The concluding remarks of the author.] The rules of the "dispensations" have been briefly presented here.

Sufism consists of states and stations, ethical qualities, and rules of conduct, and "dispensations." The dispensations are the lowest of these [three categories]. He who adheres to the

---

(Jīlānī, I, 49). He states that there are two opinions on this matter: one approving of this practice and the other disapproving. Jīlānī himself opines that it is better *not* to scatter the food but to distribute it nicely among the guests.

totality [of the Sufi doctrine] is one of those who follow the reality. He who adheres to the external aspect, namely, the ethical qualities and the rules of conduct, is one of those who follow the external custom. He who adheres to the dispensations and accepts the rules which govern them is one of the truthful simulators, about whom the Prophet said: "Whoever makes the effort to resemble a group of people is one of them." This is so, if he observes the three essential principles. The Sufi masters are unanimous in asserting that to violate these principles or one of them is to transgress the rules of Sufism. These principles are: to perform the religious duties, to avoid that which is forbidden, and to relinquish worldly possessions, except what is absolutely necessary. Such necessities are those things which the Prophet excluded from the definition of worldly goods in his saying: "There are four things which are of this world and yet are not of it: a piece of bread to satisfy your hunger, a piece of cloth (*khirqa*) to cover your nakedness, a house to shelter you from the cold and the heat, and a virtuous wife whom you can trust." The Sufi has no right to possess anything more than these four things. Junayd was asked, "What do you say about a person whose worldly possessions are no more than 'a sucking of a date stone'? Can the name of Sufism be applied to him?" He said: "The *mukātab*[83] is a slave as long as he owes [his master] a single dirham."

Whoever adopts the dispensations is one of the beginners, and he should strive to enhance his inner state and ascend to the heights of the *aḥwāl*. Whoever falls below the level of the "dispensations" thereby renounces Sufism and is forbidden to enjoy the gifts and endowments which are made for the Sufis, and the Sufi congregation should excommunicate him.

208. [Final prayer by the author.] May God in His gracious

[83] *Mukātab* is a slave who made a contract with his master to buy back his freedom from him; see *EI*², s.v. "ʿAbd" (vol. I, p. 30).

favor count us among the truthful and join us to those who seek Reality. May He preserve us from base actions both outward and inward, and enable us to seek His pleasure, both hidden and revealed. May He cause us and all Muslims to benefit from this our compilation, and may He not permit it to bring harm either to us or to those who study it. In His gracious compassion, may He not make it our lot to have compiled and memorized it without practicing and observing it. He, great is His name, is near and responsive.

Bibliography

Abū Nuʿaym al-Iṣfahānī, Aḥmad b. ʿAbdallāh. *Ḥilyat al-Awliyāʾ wa-Ṭabaqāt al-Aṣfiyāʾ*. 10 vols. in 5. Cairo: Maktabat al-Khānjī wa-Maṭbaʿat Miṣr, 1932–1938.

Anawati, G.—C., and L. Gardet. *Mystique musulmane*. Paris: J. Vrin, 1961.

Arberry, Arthur J. *An Introduction to the History of Sufism*. The Sir Abdullah Suhrawardy Lectures for 1942. London: Longmans, Green and Co., 1942.

——— *Sufism: An Account of the Mystics of Islam*. London: George Allen and Unwin, Ltd., 1950.

——— *The Doctrine of the Ṣūfis*. A translation of *Kitāb al-taʿarruf li-madhhab ahl al-taṣawwuf* by Abū Bakr al-Kalābādhī. Cambridge: Cambridge University Press, 1935.

al-Baghawī, Abū Muḥammad al-Ḥusayn. *Maṣābīḥ al-Sunna*. Cairo, n. d.

Bākharzī, Abū al-Mafākhir Yaḥyā. *Awrād al-Aḥbāb wa-Fuṣūṣ al-Ādāb*, ed. Īraj Afshār. Teheran: Publications de l'Université de Téhéran, 1966.

Brockelmann, Carl. *Geschichte der Arabischen Literatur*. 2 vols. 2nd ed. Leiden: E. J. Brill, 1943–1949. (Cited: *GAL*.)

——— *Geschichte der Arabischen Literatur*, 3 Supplementary volumes. Leiden: E. J. Brill, 1937–1949. (Cited: *GAL Supp.*)

al-Dhahabī, Shams al-Dīn Muḥammad. "*Tārīkh al-Islām*." Oxford, Bodleian Library MS. Laud. Or. 304.

Encyclopaedia of Islam, The. 4 vols. and supplement. Leiden: E. J. Brill, and London: Luzac & Co., 1913–1938. New edition, 1960–.

al-Ghazālī, Abū Ḥāmid Muḥammad b. Muḥammad. *Iḥyāʾ ʿUlūm al-Dīn*. 4 vols. Cairo: Muṣṭafā al-Bābī al-Ḥalabī, 1358/1939.

al-Ghazālī, Aḥmad. *Bawāriq al-Ilmāʿ*, ed. James Robson, in Robson, *Tracts on Listening to Music* (London, 1938). See under Robson.

Gibb, Hamilton A. R. *Mohammedanism*. 2nd ed. London: Oxford University Press, 1964.

——— *Studies on the Civilization of Islam*, ed. Stanford J. Shaw and William R. Polk. Boston: Beacon Press, 1962.

——— and Harold Bowen. *Islamic Society and the West*. Vol. I, Part II. London: Oxford University Press, 1957.

al-Ḥalabī, ʿAlī b. Burhān al-Dīn. *Insān al-ʿUyūn fī Sīrat al-Amīn wa'l-Ma'mūn*, known as *Al-Sīra al-Ḥalabiyya*. Cairo: Al-Maṭbaʿa al-Tijāriyya, n.d.

al-Hujwīrī, ʿAlī b. ʿUthmān. *Kashf al-Maḥjūb*, trans. R. A. Nicholson. E. J. W. Gibb Memorial Series, vol. XVII. Leiden: E. J. Brill and London: Luzac & Co., 1911.

Ibn al-Athīr, ʿIzz al-Dīn Abū al-Ḥasan ʿAlī. *Al-Kāmil fī al-Tārīkh*. 13 vols. Beirut: Dār Ṣādir, 1966. (The Beirut edition was reprinted from the edition of Tornberg [Leiden, 1853–1864].)

Ibn Baṭṭūṭa. *Riḥlat Ibn Baṭṭūṭa*. Beirut: Dār Ṣādir, 1960.

——— *The Travels of Ibn Baṭṭūṭa*, trans. H. A. R. Gibb. Vol. II. Published for the Hakluyt Society. Cambridge: Cambridge University Press, 1962.

Ibn al-ʿImād, Abū al-Falāḥ ʿAbd al-Ḥayy. *Shadharāt al-Dhahab fī Akhbār Man Dhahab*. Cairo: Maktabat al-Qudsī, 1931–1932.

Ibn al-Jawzī, Abū al-Faraj ʿAbd al-Raḥmān b. ʿAlī. *Al-Muntaẓam fī Tārīkh al-Mulūk wa'l-Umam*. 6 vols. (V-X). Hyderabad: Osmania Oriental Publishing Bureau, 1938–1939.

——— *Talbīs Iblīs*. Cairo: Maṭbaʿat al-Saʿāda, 1340 A.H.

Ibn Kathīr, ʿImād al-Dīn Abu al-Fidā' Ismāʿīl. *Al-Bidāya wa'l-Nihāya fī al-Tārīkh*. Cairo: Matbaʿat al-Saʿāda, n.d.

Ibn Khallikān, *Wafayāt al-Aʿyān wa-Anbā' Abnā' al-Zamān*. Cairo: Maṭbaʿat al-Nahḍa, 1947.

——— *Ibn Khallikan's Biographical Dictionary*, trans. Baron MacGuckin De Slane. 4 vols. Paris and London, 1842–1871.

al-Jīlānī, ʿAbd al-Qādir. *Al-Ghunya li-Ṭālibī Ṭariq al-Ḥaqq*. 2 vols. in one. Cairo: Muṣṭafā al-Bābī al-Ḥalabī, 1375/1956.

Jāmī, ʿAbd al-Raḥmān b. Aḥmad. *Nafaḥāt al-Uns*. Teheran, 1336 (A.H. solar calendar)/1957.

al-Kalābādhī, Abū Bakr. *Kitāb al-Taʿarruf li-Madhhab Ahl al-Taṣawwuf*. Cairo, 1960. This edition appears to be based on Arberry's edition of 1935.)

Kissling, H. J. "Aus der Geschichte des Chalvetijje Ordens," *Zeitschrift der Deutschen Morgenländischen Gesellschaft*, 103 (1953), 233–289.

al-Kubrā, Najm al-Dīn. *Fawā'iḥ al-Jamāl wa-Fawātiḥ al-Jalāl*, ed. F. Meier in Meier, *Die Fawā'iḥ al-Ǧamāl wa-Fawātiḥ al Ǧalāl des Naǧm ad-Dīn al Kubrā*. (Wiesbaden, Franz Steiner Verlag, 1957). See under Meier.

Makdisi, George. *Ibn ʿAqīl et la résurgence de l'Islam traditionaliste au XIe siècle.* Damascus: Institut Français de Damas, 1963.

——— "Muslim Institutions of Learning in Eleventh Century Baghdad," *Bulletin of the School of Oriental and African Studies*, 24 (1961), 1–56.

al-Makkī, Abū Ṭālib Muḥammad b. ʿAlī. *Qūt al-Qulūb.* 2 vols. Cairo: Muṣṭafā al-Bābī al-Ḥalabī, 1381/1961.

Massignon, Louis. *La Passion d'al-Ḥallāj.* 2 vols. Paris: P. Geuthner, 1922.

——— Essai sur les origines du lexique technique de la mystique musulmane. New and revised ed. Paris: J. Vrin, 1954.

Meier, Fritz. *Die Fawā'iḥ al-Ǧamāl wa-Fawātiḥ al-Ǧalāl des Naǧm ad-Dīn al-Kubrā.* Akademie der Wissenschaften und der Literatur; Veröffentlichungen der Orientalischen Comission, vol. IX. Wiesbaden: Franz Steiner Verlag, 1957.

——— "Der Derwischtanz, Versuch eines Überblickes," *Asiatischen Studien* (Bern), 8 (1954), 107–136.

———"Ein Knigge für Sufi's," *Revista degli Studi Orientali*, 32 (1957), 485–524.

Molé, Marijan. *Les Mystiques musulmans.* Paris: Presses Universitaires de France, 1965.

al-Qushayrī, Abū al-Qāsim, ʿAbd al-Karīm. *Al-Risāla al-Qushayriyya.* Cairo: Muṣṭafā al-Bābī al-Ḥalabī, 1379/1959.

Ritter, Hellmut. "Philologika IX: Die vier Suhrawardī," *Der Islam*, 25 (1939), 35–86.

Robson, James, ed. and trans. *Tracts on Listening to Music* (*Dhamm al-malāhī* by Ibn Abī'l-Dunyā and *Bawāriq al-Ilmāʿ* by Majd al-Dīn al Ṭūsī al-Ghazālī.) Oriental Translation Fund, n.s. vol. XXXIV. London: Royal Asiatic Society, 1938.

al-Ṣafadī, Khalīl b. Aybak. *Al-Wāfī bi'l-Wafayāt.* Vol. I, ed. Hellmut Ritter, Wiesbaden, 1962. Vols. II-III, ed. S. Dedering, Istanbul, 1949–1953.

al-Samʿānī, Abū Saʿd ʿAbd al-Karīm. "Kitāb al-Ansāb." MS, Istanbul, Köprülü 1010.

al-Sarrāj, Abū Naṣr. *Kitāb al-Lumaʿ fī al-Taṣawwuf*, ed. R. A. Nicholson. E. J. W. Gibb Memorial Series, vol. XXII. Leiden: E. J. Brill, and London: Luzac & Co., 1914.

Scholem, Gershom G. *Major Trends in Jewish Mysticism.* London: Thames & Hudson, 1955.

Setton, K. M., and M. W. Baldwin, eds. *A History of the Crusades.* Vol. I. Philadelphia: University of Pennsylvania Press, 1958.

al-Shaʿrānī, ʿAbd al-Wahhāb. *Al-Anwār al-Qudsiyya fī Maʿrifat Qawāʿid al-Ṣufiyya.* 2 vols. Cairo: al-Maktaba al-ʿIlmiyya, 1962.

Shaykh-Zādeh, ʿAbd al-Raḥīm b. ʿAlī. *Naẓm al-Farāʾid wa-Jamʿ al-Fawāʾid.* Cairo, n.d.

Siddiqi, Amir Hasan. *Caliphate and Sultanate.* 2nd ed. Karachi: Jamiyat-ul-Falah, 1963.

Sibṭ Ibn al-Jawzī. *Mirʾāt al-Zamān*, ed. James R. Jewett (a facsimile edition of part VIII). Chicago: The University of Chicago Press, 1907.

al-Subkī, Tāj al-Dīn Abū Naṣr. *Ṭabaqāt al-Shāfiʿiyya al-Kubrā.* Cairo: Al-Maṭbaʿa al-Ḥusayniyya, [1323–24/1905–06].

al-Suhrawardī, Abū Ḥafṣ ʿUmar Shihāb al-Dīn. *ʿAwārif al-Maʿārif.* Beirut: Dār al-Kitāb al-ʿArabī, 1966.

al-Sulamī, Abū ʿAbd al-Raḥmān. *Kitāb Ādāb al-Ṣuḥba*, ed. M. J. Kister. Jerusalem: Israel Oriental Society, 1954.

——— *Kitāb Ṭabaqāt al-Ṣūfiyya*, ed. J. Pedersen. Leiden, 1960.

———*Jawāmiʿ Ādāb al-Ṣūfiyya and ʿUyūb al-Nafs wa-Mudāwātuhā*, ed. E. Kohlberg. Jerusalem: The Institute of Asian and African Studies, The Hebrew University of Jerusalem.

Talas, Asad. *L'Enseignement chez les Arabes: La Madrasa Nizamiyya et son histoire.* Paris: P. Geuthner, 1939.

Trimingham, J. Spencer. *The Sufi Orders in Islam.* Oxford: Oxford University Press, 1971.

Wensinck, A. J. *The Muslim Creed.* Cambridge: Cambridge University Press, 1932.

——— et al. *Concordance et indices de la tradition musulmane.* Leiden: E. J. Brill, 1936–.

al-Yāfiʿī, Abū Muḥammad ʿAbdallāh. *Mirʾāt al-Janān wa-ʿIbrat al-Yaqẓān.* Hyderabad, 1338 A.H.

Yāqūt, Shihāb al-Dīn Abū ʿAbdallāh. *Kitāb Muʿjam al-Buldān*, ed. Wüstenfeld. Leipzig, 1868. (German title: *Jacut's Geographisches Wörterbuch.*)

——— *Muʿjam al-Udabāʾ*. 20 vols. in 10. Cairo: Dār al-Maʾmūn, 1936–1938.

Glossary

The references are given in this Glossary by page for the Introduction and by section for the Abridged Translation. The article (*al*) is disregarded in the alphabetic arrangement.

ʿabd, slave, a common designation of man in relation to God, p. 2
adab (pl. *ādāb*), rule of conduct, proper conduct, ethics, pp. 16, 21, 25, secs. 2, 42, 44, 68, 76, 134; cultural formation, sec. 43; literature, belles-lettres, pp. 12, 21, 23, 24
ahl al-ṣuffa, the "people of the portico," sec. 166. *See also* sec. 40
ahl ṣuḥbatihi, members of one's brotherhood, sec. 168. See also *ṣuḥba*
ahl al-sunna wa-'l-jamāʿa, literally, "those who adhere to the tradition and the community," the orthodox, p. 6
aḥwāl (see sing. *ḥāl*), pp. 5, 17, secs. 37, 38, 39, 41, 50, 51, 72, 95, 207
ʿālim (pl. *ʿulamā'*), a learned man, a man of religious learning (*ʿilm*), sec. 59
ʿamal, praxis (as the counterpart of religious knowledge, *ʿilm*), secs. 33, 39, 52, 59
al-ʿāmma (pl. *al-ʿawāmm*), the common people, the vulgar, sec. 57
ʿaql, intellect, secs. 53, 59
ʿārif (pl. *ʿārifūn*), he who knows. In Sufism, the term signifying him who is possessed of *maʿrifa* (mystical knowledge), secs. 39, 71, 132, 143
ʿārifūn (see sing. *ʿārif*), p. 25, sec. 21
al-arkān, "the pillars," the five essential duties of Islam, sec. 13
aṣḥāb al-ḥadīth, the traditionists, those learned in the science of Ḥadīth, sec. 34
ʿawāmm (see sing. *al-ʿāmma*), sec. 99
ʿazā'im, pl. of *ʿazīma* which signifies "a rule in its strict interpretation," the opposite of *rukhṣa*, sec. 166

balā', affliction, trial, secs. 163, 165

baraka, divine blessing or grace, "mana," secs. 117, 121, 129, 151
bāṭin, internal (esoteric) aspect, sec. 41
ḍarūra, necessity (which justifies the relaxation of rules), sec. 170
darwīsh (Persian), mendicant, a term signifying an ordinary Sufi, p. 9
dhāt, essence, sec. 3
dhikr, remembrance of God, recitation of God's names, secs. 92, 122, 135; Sufi assemblies dedicated to such recitations, pp. 8, 9, 13, 15

faqīr (pl. *fuqarā'*), a poor man, a term signifying an ordinary Sufi, p. 9, secs. 126, 147
faqr, poverty, sec. 16; poverty, as one of the Sufi stations, p. 9, sec. 49. *See also* sec. 17
faraḥ, joy (occurring as a result of Sufi audition), sec. 30
farā'iḍ, obligatory rituals, sec. 132
fāsiq, sinner, sec. 13
fawātiḥ, revealed signs, sec. 50
fiqh, Islamic jurisprudence, pp. 12, 13, 14, sec. 98
fuqahā' (sing. *faqīh*), those learned in *fiqh* (jurisprudence), p. 14, secs. 34, 35
fuqarā' (see sing. *faqīr*), p. 9, secs. 126, 147
futuwwa, chivalry, sec. 103

ghafla, headlessness; in Sufism, signifying the state of a person whose spirit is not religiously awake, sec. 61
ghayba, absence of selfhood, sec. 32
ghurabā' (sing. *gharīb*), those who are away from their home, sec. 84

ḥāl (pl. *aḥwāl*), state (a transitory mental state), secs. 30, 57, 72. *See also* sec. 50
ḥaqīqa, esoteric true reality, pp. 6, 7, secs. 39, 146
al-ḥaqq, the Real One, one of the names of God especially favored by the Sufis, secs. 41, 147
ḥayā', diffidence, one of the Sufi states, sec. 50
himma, ambition; in Sufism, religious ambition, secs. 32, 44, 113
ḥuzn, grief, one of the Sufi states, sec. 30

ikhlāṣ, sincerity, one of the Sufi stations, sec. 49
'ilm, knowledge in general, sec. 59; religious learning, especially learning of the holy law, p. 26, secs. 33, 39, 52, 53, 58, 59, 98, 113
imām, the leader of public prayer, sec. 8
īmān, faith, correct religious belief, sec. 13

ināba, returning, one of the Sufi stations, sec. 49
inbisāṭ, informality, the opposite of *takalluf*, sec. 126
irāda, aspiration, p. 18; aspiration as one of the Sufi stations, sec. 49
isnād, chain of authorities transmitting a tradition from the Prophet, p. 23
istibshār, delight (occurring as a result of Sufi audition), sec. 30
iṣṭilām, loss of consciousness (as a symptom of ecstasy), sec. 32
istithnā', the use of the conditional expression "if Allah will it," p. 21, sec. 14
īthār, altruism, secs. 76, 129

jamʿ al-himma, concentration of religious ambition, sec. 32. See also *himma*

kāfir, unbeliever, sec. 13
kā'in, generated being, sec. 3
karāma (pl. *karāmāt*), divine grace, miracle performed by a Sufi saint (divine grace as demonstrated by such a miracle), sec. 23
khādim, servant, a term signifying the Steward of a Sufi brotherhood, secs. 157, 100n
khawf, fear, one of the Sufi states, secs. 30, 32, 50
khidma, service, signifying here the office of the *khādim*, sec. 100
khidmat al-ikhwān, service to one's brethren, sec. 78
khirqa (pl. *khiraq*), literally, a piece of cloth or a rag; the standard term for the Sufi mantle, p. 26, secs. 148, 149, 150, 151, 207

madrasa, Islamic college for the study of the holy law, pp. 13, 15
maghrib, the sunset prayer (the first of two prayers performed after sunset), sec. 133
maḥabba, love as a characteristic of lay members, p. 18; love as a Sufi state, secs. 32, 50
maqām (pl. *maqāmāt*), station (in the Sufi way), pp. 3, 5, 17, secs. 37, 38, 41, 49, 68, 72
maʿrifa, mystical knowledge, gnosis, secs. 53, 59
mawjūd, existent being, sec. 3
mubtadiʿ, innovator, a person acting not in accordance with the established practice (*sunna*), sec. 13
muftī, Muslim jurisconsult, p. 15
muḥāsabat al-nafs, examination of the soul, one of the Sufi stations, sec. 49
muḥāwara, conversation, signifying the communication of Sufi doctrine, sec. 54
muḥibbūn, lovers, a term applied to lay members, p. 19, sec. 151
muḥrim, a consecrated pilgrim, sec. 118

mu'jizāt, miracles of prophets, sec. 23
mu'min, believer, true Muslim, sec. 14
munāfiq, hypocrite, sec. 13
muntahin, consummate Sufi, sec. 40
murāqaba, attentive observation, one of the Sufi states, sec. 50
muraqqa'a (pl. *muraqqa'āt*), the patched frock of the Sufi, secs. 25, 66, 151, 177, 193
murīd (pl. *murīdūn*), aspirant, a term signifying the novice in Sufism, pp. 8, 18, 25, secs. 39, 40, 61, 62, 66, 67, 68, 71, 73, 75, 143
mushāhada, vision of the divine power (as the ultimate Sufi state), sec. 50
mutashabbihūn, simulators, those who earnestly try to resemble the Sufis (lay members), p. 18; false simulators, sec. 47
mutawassiṭ, (pl. *mutawassiṭun*), Sufi of intermediate rank, p. 25, secs. 39, 40, 71

nafs, the lower soul, secs. 44, 49, 63, 73, 74, 158
nawāfil, (sing. *nāfila*), supererogatory prayers, sec. 132

qurb, nearness, one of the Sufi states, sec. 50

al-rabb, God, the Master, p. 2
rajā', hope, one of the Sufi states, secs. 30, 32, 50
rak'a, literally, bowing; a set cycle of movements and recitations forming a unit in the ritual prayer, each prayer consisting of a certain number of such "bowings," secs. 110, 133
ribāṭ, a Sufi convent, p. 13
riḍā, pleasure (God's) or satisfaction (man's), sec. 19; satisfaction, one of the Sufi stations, sec. 49
riyāḍāt, exercises of self-discipline, sec. 87
ruḥ, spirit (as the opposite of *nafs*, the lower soul), secs. 31, 74
rukhṣa (pl. *rukhaṣ*), dispensation or relaxation of the strict rule, pp. 17, 19, 20, secs. 140, 166–206
ru'yat allāh, beatific vision (that is, seeing Allah in paradise), sec. 6

ṣabr, patience, one of the Sufi stations, sec. 49
samā', Sufi audition, pp. 8, 19, 25, secs. 28, 29, 31, 32, 135–138, 140, 142–149, 151, 174
sharī'a, the divine law, pp. 2, 3, 6, 7, secs. 25, 33, 48
shaṭḥiyyāt, ecstatic utterances, sec. 57
shawq, yearning, as one of the Sufi states, secs. 30, 50

shaykh, Sufi master, p. 8, et passim. (After the first occurrence, set in roman type)
ṣiddīqūn, saints, sec. 21
ṣidq, veracity, one of the Sufi stations, sec. 49
ṣifāt, the attributes of God, sec. 3
sirr, secret, sec. 32; signifying the innermost element of the heart, sec. 43
ṣūf, wool, p. 4
ṣūfī (pl. *ṣūfiyya*), Sufi, p. 4, et passim (set in roman type)
ṣuḥba, companionship, secs. 76, 98, 101, 198
sukhṭ, God's wrath, sec. 19
sunna, established commendable custom (regarded as derived from the practice of the Prophet), p. 19, secs. 130, 152, 162
sunnī, following the *sunna*, hence orthodox, p. 6

takalluf, affected manner, formal behavior (the opposite of *inbisāṭ*), secs. 103, 111
ṭarab, rapture (as inspired by *samāʿ*), sec. 32
ṭarīqa, the mystical way, pp. 5, 8, 9, 10; a Sufi order, p. 10
taṣabbur, forbearance, one of the Sufi stations, sec. 49
taṣawwuf, Sufism, p. 4, sec. 17
tawājud, artificial ecstasy, sec. 146
tawakkul, trust in God, p. 9; as one of the Sufi stations, sec. 49
tawba, repentance, secs. 49, 64
ta'wīlāt, esoteric interpretations, p. 20, sec. 36
ṭuma'nīna, serenity, one of the Sufi states, sec. 50

ʿulamā' (see sing. *ʿālim*), pp. 6, 13, secs. 10, 33, 52
al-umma, the community of Islam, p. 2
uns, intimacy, one of the Sufi states, sec. 50
ustādh, Sufi master, shaykh, sec. 82

wajd, ecstatic yearning, ecstasy, secs. 32, 146
waqt, moment, momentary experience, secs. 40, 42
waraʿ, scrupulosity, p. 3, secs. 49, 65, 68

yaqīn, certainty, one of the Sufi states, sec. 50

ẓāhir, the exoteric aspect of Sufism, sec. 41
zuhd, asceticism, pp. 3, 4, sec. 48; renunciation, one of the Sufi stations, p. 3, secs. 49, 66, 68

Harvard Middle Eastern Studies

Out of print titles are omitted

3. *The Idea of the Jewish State.* By Ben Halpern. 1961. (Second edition, 1969.)

4. *The Agricultural Policy of Muhammad'Ali in Egypt.* By Helen Anne B. Rivlin. 1961.

5. *Egypt in Search of Political Community: An Analysis of the Intellectual and Political Evolution of Egypt 1804–1952.* By Nadav Safran. 1961 (also a Harvard Political Study).

6. *The Economy of Cyprus.* By A. J. Meyer, with Simos Vassiliou. 1962.*

7. *Entrepreneurs of Lebanon: The Role of the Business Leader in a Developing Economy.* By Yusif A. Sayigh. 1962.*

8. *The Opening of South Lebanon, 1788–1840: A Study of the Impact of the West on the Middle East.* By William R. Polk. 1963.

9. *The First Turkish Republic: A Case Study in National Development.* By Richard Robinson. 1963.

10. *The Armenian Communities in Syria under Ottoman Dominion.* By Avedis K. Sanjian. 1965.

12. *Tripoli: A Modern Arab City.* By John Gulick. 1967.

13. *Pioneers East: The Early American Experience in the Middle East.* By David H. Finnie. 1967.

14. *Shaykh and Effendi: Changing Patterns of Authority Among the El Shabana of Southern Iraq.* By Robert A. Fernea. 1970.

15. *Between Old and New: The Ottoman Empire under Sultan Selim III, 1789–1807.* By Stanford J. Shaw. 1971.

16. *The Patricians of Nishapur: A Study in Medieval Islamic Social History.* By Richard W. Bulliet. 1972.

17. *A Sufi Rule for Novices: Kitāb Ādāb al-Murīdīn.* By Menahem Milson. 1975.

*Published jointly by the Center for International Affairs and the Center for Middle Eastern Studies.

†Published jointly by the Center for Middle Eastern Studies and the Joint Center for Urban Studies.